Hollywood According to Hollywood

Other Books by A l e x   B a r r i s

The Pierce Arrow Showroom is Leaking

Hollywood's Other Men

Hollywood's Other Women

Stop The Presses!

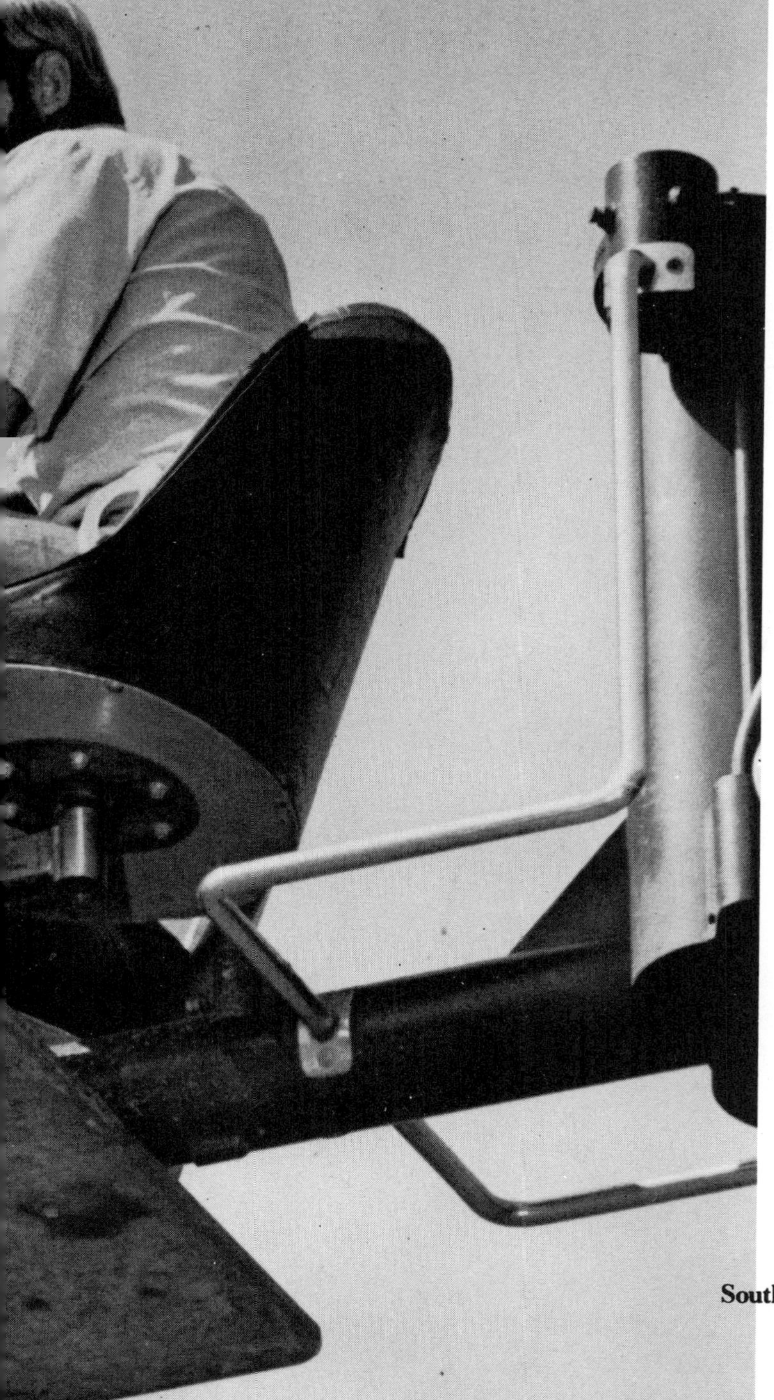

Hollywood According to Hollywood

Alex Barris

South Brunswick and New York: A. S. Barnes and Company

London: Thomas Yoseloff Ltd

A. S. Barnes and Co., Inc.
Cranbury, New Jersey 08512

Thomas Yoseloff Ltd
Magdalen House
136-148 Tooley Street
London SE1 2TT, England

Library of Congress Cataloging in Publication Data

Barris, Alex.
    Hollywood according to Hollywood.

    Includes index.
    1. Moving-picture industry in motion pictures.
2. Moving-pictures—United States. I. Title.
PN1995.9.M65B3   791.43'0909'372   75-38435
ISBN 0-498-01748-6

To Kay,
my favorite wife

Contents

Introduction

In a 1951 potboiler, entitled *Hollywood Story,* the late Richard Conte played a movie producer bent on making a film about an unsolved 1929 murder of a famed Hollywood director. To the surprise of virtually no one, he not only forged ahead with his movie idea, but ended up solving the old murder mystery as well.

Jim Backus played an agent in *Hollywood Story,* and also served as an intermittent narrator for the movie. In an early scene, he tried to dissuade Conte from his purpose on the ground that Hollywood stories were not what the public wanted.

"Backstage stories are okay," Backus was required to argue, "but back-camera stories are absolutely no good."

With regard to the particular back-camera story Conte was trying to construct, Backus may have been right, because *Hollywood Story* — although allegedly based on the actual unsolved murder (in 1921) of a silent screen era director named William Desmond Taylor — emerged as a routine B-picture, devoid of any style or other distinction.

But as a professional agent's appraisal of what constituted good box office, Backus's advice was patently worthless. For the fact is, as it was in 1951, that Hollywood stories, if not this particular *Hollywood Story,* can often be very good box office.

In the roughly sixty-year history of feature films, there have been hundreds of movies that dealt with Hollywood — and very few of them needed as obvious an excuse as a murder mystery to support them.

True, not every one of these has been a box-office smash, but, then, a lot of them did not deserve to rake in millions of dollars. On the other hand, a great many of them were commercial successes; some were artistic successes, too — including *Sunset Boulevard,* which was made just the year before *Hollywood Story* and may, indeed, have provided the impetus for basing a film on the long-forgotten mystery of the murdered Mr. Taylor.

Hollywood's fascination with Hollywood began not long after America's fascination with Hollywood did, and that means not long after the star system was born.

The early movie tycoons treated their leading players like any other employees, and insisted on keeping them anonymous. Florence Lawrence, one of the popular players of the first decade of this century, was known only as "the Biograph girl," that being the studio that made her films, until she insisted on some recognition and switched studios to implement her demands. Even Mary Pickford, the greatest star of her era, was billed merely as

"Little Mary" until the public demanded more information.

It was the public, really, that created the star system, rather than the studios. Captivated by the screen personalities of Little Mary and other early players, moviegoers wanted to know more about them. And the studio heads gradually recognized that they had created, or had forced upon them, a very marketable commodity — The Star. It was as if someone had gone into the business of making and selling doughnuts and only later realized that the dough punched out to create the hole could be used to make more doughnuts.

With the studio publicity departments grinding out material, the willing help of the burgeoning fan magazines, and the seemingly insatiable appetite of movie fans for more and more information about their favorite stars, Hollywood created a kind of fairy-tale American royalty, an endless parade of dazzling, magical personalities whose every step was chronicled in newspaper gossip columns and slick paper magazine stories; whose taste in food, dress, colors, hobbies, and members of the opposite sex became as familiar to millions of Americans as the life-style of the Royal Family was to Britons.

Thus, having tripped over the fact that Americans were not only movie crazy, but mesmerized by the stars who made the movies, the studios took the next logical step — beating their own drums, capitalizing on the "glamorous" appeal of Hollywood's most famous industry.

Well before sound came to movies, the filmmakers had begun to dabble in Hollywood themes — some frivolous, some blatantly sentimental, some fairly compelling. In the decades that followed, the film studios collectively have provided a sort of history of Hollywood, often spurious and sugar-coated, to be sure, but occasionally revealing a bit of "the real tinsel," as one cynic put it, that hides the phoney tinsel of Hollywood.

In other industries, huge corporations spend millions of dollars on public relations, creating a suitable "public image" of themselves, their products, and their importance to the fabric of American life.

In the movie industry, the very cameras, sets, lights, producers, directors, designers, writers, and actors who have always supplied the "product" were, from time to time, put to use publicizing, mythologizing, glamorizing Hollywood.

Not surprisingly, the vast majority of movies dealing with Hollywood and moviemaking bore no more relation to reality than did the majority of Hollywood movies that dealt with life, love, war, crime, or, for that matter, the biographies of noted persons.

But that did not stop millions of movie fans from paying billions of dollars to see these films whenever they came along. And even though that Hollywood is now generally regarded as being "dead," the fact is that filmmakers, both in and out of Hollywood, are currently riding on a wave of nostalgia that is bringing forth movies about movie people at a greater rate than ever before.

So it would appear that the agent played by Jim Backus in *Hollywood Story* was wrong not only then, but now and for the forseeable future as well.

Hollywood According to Hollywood

1 Hollywood in the Spotlight

Before filmmakers were sufficiently bold to attempt full-length features, and before audiences became conditioned to accept the longer screen form, the short subject was the movie industry's primary product.

Once the novelty of "moving pictures" had worn off, and filmmakers had developed ways of telling longer, fuller stories that could yet sustain audience interest, the feature film became the Hollywood staple, and short subjects were offered as "added attractions" to round out a program.

Similarly, before feature pictures began using the Hollywood glamor legend as a backdrop for story-telling, short subjects were being made in which the studios used the studios, and their players, to feed the audience's growing hunger for anything and everything concerning moviemaking and its attendant "magic."

A generation or more before Marshall McLuhan ever coined the phrase, Hollywood was already practicing his theory that "the medium is the message." That is, the medium was being used, at times, merely to perpetuate the medium — that was the message.

In 1919, Jack Cohn, brother of the more famous Harry Cohn (head of Columbia Studios, and its founder), conceived the idea of a "screen fan magazine" to present filmed glimpses of the stars at work and play. To put this plan into effect, he teamed with brother Harry and with Joe Brandt to form what soon became Columbia Pictures. That was the studio that, for some thirty years, turned out the most durable series of film shorts dealing with the stars — "Screen Snapshots." This series, for a long time under the stewardship of Ralph Staub, lasted until 1958 and, in its peak years (1935 to 1945), came up with as many as twenty one-reel "Screen Snapshots" in a year.

Even before Screen Snapshots, Staub turned out a one-reeler called *Screen Star Sports* that showed, among other things, Myrna Loy and Bessie Love playing *bocce,* the Italian variation of lawn bowling. Staub was also responsible for *Jimmy Fidler's Personality Parade,* using that well-known gossip columnist's reputation for reporting on the stars. And Harriet Parsons, daughter of the redoubtable Louella, produced and narrated a series of shorts called *Meet the Stars.* Miss Parsons was later involved with the *Screen Snapshots* series.

Making movies about movies (even short ones) had been done before Staub, Parsons, and Jack Cohn began delving into Hollywood background. Back in 1916, when Harold Lloyd was making short comedies for Pathe as "Lonesome Luke," one of these had dealt with moviemaking.

And some of Charlie Chaplin's early short films

The Studio Rube. Onetime Keystone Cop Al St. John is about to get into trouble as a novice in a movie studio. (Fox, 1924)

The Hollywood Kid. That's Cecille Evand and Gordon Lewis on the diving board, watched by a bevy of Sennett bathing beauties. (Mack Sennett, 1924)

climbed on the Hollywood bandwagon, too. In 1915, when he was working for Essanay, he made *His New Job,* which took place in a movie studio. So did *Behind the Screen,* which Chaplin made the following year.

In the latter film, Chaplin was a bumbling stagehand in a film studio, creating marvelous chaos with props, tripping over cameras, being overworked and underthanked while most of his colleagues loafed. The climax of this two-reeler featured a mass pie-throwing battle, with Chaplin pitted against a succession of his tormenters.

Al St. John, who had been one of the Keystone Cops (along with Chaplin, Fatty Arbuckle, Ford Sterling, Hank Mann, and others) made a short for Fox in 1924 called *The Studio Rube,* in which he created comic chaos on a movie set.

At about the same time, Mack Sennett came up with *The Hollywood Kid,* a humorous look at the glamorous life, with Cecille Evans and Gordon Lewis. Other shorts of the 1920s that sought to

The top image is a lobby card.

The Hollywood Handicap. Don Alvarado starred in this short about a cross-country auto race ending in Hollywood. (Carl Laemmle, 1925)

Hazel From Hollywood. A lobby card advertising this early short subject set in a film studio. (Educational Pictures, 1925)

capitalize on the public's growing fascination with the movie business included *Hazel From Hollywood,* with Dorothy Devore and Henry Murdock, and *The Hollywood Handicap,* with a group called The Thalians and Don Alvarado.

In the 1930s, Carey Wilson narrated many short subjects for MGM. One of them was *Extra, Extra,* which purported to give the public some insight into the trials and tribulations of life as a movie extra. Also in that decade, Robert Benchley, another MGM favorite in short subjects before he became an actor in features, appeared in a short called *A Night at the Movies,* which presented Benchley running into all kinds of problems while seeking an evening's entertainment.

The same studio turned out a series called *The Romance of Celluloid* — a singularly uninspired title — giving the public behind-the-scenes glimpses of how various cinematic effects were achieved. One of them, called *Power,* showed how the International Ice Follies' skaters were filmed for an

Extra, Extra. **This Carey Wilson short sought to focus on the rough life of movie extras. (MGM, circa 1933)**

A Night at the Movies. **Only Robert Benchley (in derby) could make going to the movies such a complicated but funny undertaking. (MGM, circa 1936)**

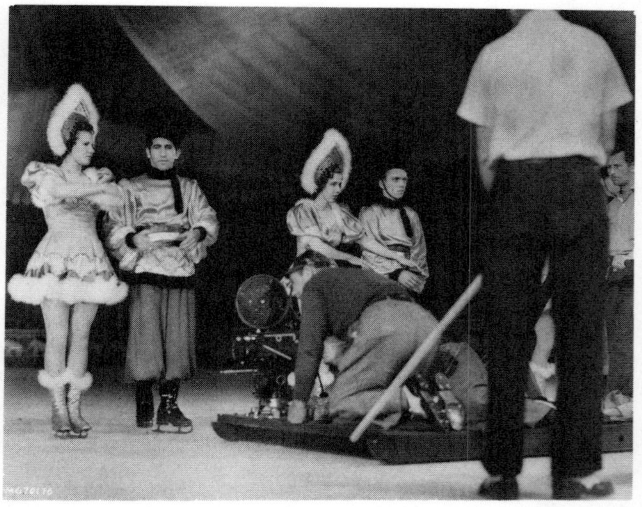

Power. **This behind-the-scenes short helped promote an upcoming feature involving the Ice Follies. (MGM, 1938)**

16

Ken Murray. This comic and shutter-bug narrated many of the *Screen Snapshots* series, was rarely photographed himself without a camera and a couple of pretty girls.

upcoming Joan Crawford movie, *The Ice Follies of 1939.*

Other studios got into the Hollywood act from time to time with short films. RKO turned out *Hollywood Light* and *Hollywood Luck,* among others. The same studio did a series called *Picture People,* more or less along the same lines as the more famous *Screen Snapshots,* and in 1942 made a short called *How to be A Star,* which had Anne Baxter (who was not one yet) in the cast. And during the Second World War, 20th Century-Fox brought out a two-reeler called *All Star Bond Rally,* and Paramount produced a short titled *Hollywood Victory Caravan.*

Even Walt Disney, by the mid-1930s undisputed king of animation, turned loose his artists on a short (in the Silly Symphony series) entitled *Mother Goose Goes Hollywood.* This one presented Katharine Hepburn as Little Bo Peep, W.C. Fields as Humpty Dumpty, and Hugh Herbert as Ole King Cole. Also in it were representations of the Marx Brothers, Laurel and Hardy, Edward G. Robinson, Charlie McCarthy, Charles Laughton, and Greta Garbo.

But the man who got the most mileage (and often the best) out of showing us candid, informal footage of Hollywood personalities was comedian Ken Murray, who appeared in and/or narrated a number of the *Screen Snapshots,* and in later years, dusted off his own substantial collection of such footage for further showings, both in theaters and on television.

Probably the first feature picture primarily concerned with the "image" of Hollywood was a 1923 film directed by James Cruze entitled *Hollywood.* While other movies were content to turn the spotlight on the film capital, this one strove to tint the light to a more soothing rose color.

The circumstances that brought it about were unusual. The public had, indeed, become aware of the glamor of Hollywood — and also of some of the less wholesome aspects of life in Hollywood. Fan magazines and sensation-seeking newspapers gave the public an image of Hollywood that some strait-laced Americans did not find to their taste. Stories of bizarre parties, excessive use of alcohol and drugs, and the highly publicized promiscuity of Hollywood stars made some people think of the film colony as being located just between Sodom and Gomorrah.

By 1921, all the news from Hollywood seemed to be bad — or at least shocking. There was the aforementioned unsolved murder of director William Desmond Taylor, with its attendant revelations about his association with two film favorites, Mabel Normand and Mary Miles Minter. In the same year, Fatty Arbuckle, until then a popular favorite, suddenly found his career in ruins after the bad publicity that followed the sordid death of Virginia Rappe at an Arbuckle party in San Francisco. As if that were not enough, Wallace Reid, another silent film star, died of an overdose of drugs in 1923.

Judged by today's standards, Hollywood movies in the early 1920s would seem bland, if not wholesome. Yet, there were those who cried out against too much sex, nudity, and other degrading elements. And these would-be censors were strengthened in their outrage by newspaper and magazine stories about the "private" lives of Hollywood's beautiful people.

Churches and other morality-minded pressure groups were calling for an end to Hollywood's excesses. Just as in the world of politics a man's private imperfections could be used to sabotage his

Mother Goose Goes Hollywood. Animation king Walt Disney let his artists loose on some famous Hollywood figures in this short. (RKO, 1936)

political aims or programs, so could the personal shortcomings of actors be used to curb their professional activities. To appease the outraged proponents of censorship, the Motion Picture Producers and Distributors of America was formed, presided over by Will Hays, once Postmaster General of the United States (under President Harding). The "Hays Office" became the arbiter of what was regarded as decent behavior in Hollywood films.

To help improve Hollywood's sullied public image, Hays decided to use the screen itself. It was at his suggestion that Cruze made the film entitled *Hollywood*. It was a mildly satirical movie in which Hope Brown went to the film capital in hopes of becoming a star — but did not. For Cruz, however, it served as a vehicle in which to sprinkle a bunch of stars and, more important, to show them in a sympathetic light. Among the stars he used were William S. Hart, Mary Pickford and Douglas Fairbanks, Charlie Chaplin, Pola Negri, Jack Holt, Will Rogers, and the ever-ready Cecil B. DeMille.

Interestingly, Fatty Arbuckle, now in disgrace, also made a brief appearance. Perhaps symbolically, he was shown at a casting director's window seeking work; the window was unceremoniously slammed shut in his face.

The Cruze film was widely acclaimed and, no doubt, helped to improve Hollywood's image. More importantly, perhaps, the Hays Office continued to hold tight rein on Hollywood products for a good many years to come.

(Eventually, Hays was succeeded by Joseph Breen, and it was the "Breen Office" that decided

Hollywood. **This James Cruze directed epic was aimed at polishing up the film colony's stained image. Above are George K. Arthur and Hope Brown. (Paramount, 1923)**

William Fox Movietone Follies of 1929. Sue Carol and David Rollins were only two of many stars in this early musical. (Fox, 1929)

what could or could not be shown in films. By the time Jack Valenti took over the post in 1966, the "production code" had been eased and/or undermined and Valenti's job became essentially a ceremonial one.)

Despite the silent shorts dealing with Hollywood in one way or another — and occasional public relations gestures like the Cruze film — it was the birth of the sound era that gave the studios their greatest impetus to really turn the spotlight on Hollywood in a big and noisy way.

Starting with the first full year of sound films (1929), the movie studios went in for large-scale blowing of their own respective horns — and Hollywood's collective one. What came out was a procession of "follies" or "revues," spotlighting the biggest stars available to each studio, in

Hollywood Revue of 1929. Those busbies on the Guards made Marion Davies look even tinier than she was. (MGM, 1929)

Hollywood Revue of 1929. Bessie Love had no choice but to listen as Marie Dressler warbled "For I'm the Queen." (MGM, 1929)

virtually plotless films designed merely to show off the stars and the new attraction of sound.

One of the first was the *William Fox Movietone Follies of 1929,* which had an onionskin plotline about the pitfalls of putting on a show, and even included the understudy who goes on for the tempermental star on opening night. Among those in the cast were Lola Lane (as the understudy), Sue Carol, De Witt Jannings, David Rollins, Stepin Fetchit, and Dixie Lee.

(Miss Lee was established as a film personality when she first met Bing Crosby, then one of Paul Whiteman's Rhythm Boys. When they married, Crosby said later, one paper headlined the story: "Well-Known Fox Movie Star Marries Bing Croveny.")

The film had a chorus line, lots of singing and dancing, some typical shuffling comedy by Mr. Fetchit, and even one sequence in the then brand-new Technicolor.

But even in 1929, as in many years to follow, the studio with the stars was MGM and they were not about to be outdone by Fox. Thus, MGM gave us *The Hollywood Revue of 1929,* with a cast that included Marion Davies, John Gilbert, Norma Shearer, William Haines, Joan Crawford, Buster Keaton, Bessie Love, Charles King, Marie Dressler, Polly Moran, Anita Page, and Gus Edwards.

When this lavish epic opened in New York, it was greeted with frequent outbursts of applause. It had not one but two sequences in Technicolor, and in one of them the faint perfume of orange blossoms filled the theater. (Shades of Smell-arama!)

Among the attractions featured was a song done by Gus Edwards entitled "Lon Chaney Will Get You If You Don't Watch Out." Marion Davies performed with a chorus of mock Grenadier Guards. Buster Keaton appeared in a funny submarine scene. Marie Dressler wowed them with "For I'm the Queen." Jack Benny and Conrad Nagel shared the job of master of ceremonies. And for the highbrows, there were Shearer and Gilbert doing the balcony scene from Romeo and Juliet. In the later words of Ira Gershwin, "who could ask for anything more?"

Warner Brothers, that's who. They wanted a piece of this appealing new pie, and they too had a roster of stars to dazzle a Hollywood-happy public. Before the year was out, Warners released *The Show of Shows,* with no less than seventy-five stars, including John Barrymore, Frank Fay, Richard Barthelmess, Beatrice Lillie, Ted Lewis, Ben Turpin, Myrna Loy, Chester Morris, H.B. Warner, Chester Conklin, Sally Eilers, and even Rin-Tin-Tin.

The Show of Shows. That's Myrna Loy in her exotic Oriental (or pre-William Powell) era. (Warner Brothers, 1929)

The Show of Shows. Frank Fay and Winnie Lightner provided one of the comic highlights of this frothy revue. (Warner Brothers, 1929)

Among other novelties, this one offered the public its first opportunity to hear (as well as see) the already legendary John Barrymore, who delivered a soliloquy as the Duke of Gloucester in Shakespeare's Henry VI. Barrymore further delighted (and possibly baffled) audiences by first appearing as himself, announcing what he was going to do, and then suddenly appearing in full costume and makeup for the role. Cinema magic, indeed.

Frank Fay and Richard Barthelmess shared the job of master of ceremonies, prizefighter Georges Carpentier did a song-and-dance turn, and Rin-Tin-Tin barked. The massive cast included two-hundred — "count 'em, two-hundred" — dancers, who miracuously managed without the guidance of the not-yet-then ubiquitous Busby Berkeley. And among the otherwise forgettable songs in the score were two gems destined to become perennial favorites: "You Were Meant For Me" and "Rockabye Your Baby With a Dixie Melody."

Gargantuanism was already setting in. In 1930, Fox came back with a larger-than-anything musical revue called *Happy Days.* This one opened at the

Happy Days. Despite the unfriendly looks of his companions, Warner Baxter (center) believes in the title. (Fox, 1930)

Happy Days. Dancer Ann Pennington and a half dozen pretties did some fancy tapping in this All-Star revue. (Fox, 1930)

famous Roxy Theater, which, for the occasion, installed a huge special screen to accommodate the film's process, modestly titled "Grandeur."

Among the Fox contract players coralled into this mock minstrel show were Warner Baxter, Janet Gaynor, Charles Farrell, Will Rogers, Victor McLaglen, Edmund Lowe, George Jessel, "Whispering Jack" Smith, Dixie Lee, El Brendel, Walter Catlett, Frank Albertson, and Ann Pennington. Oh, and just to show Warners that Carpentier was not the only fighter available to Hollywood, James J. Corbett turned up in a scene.

Flexing its technological muscles, *Happy Days* tossed in such gasp-eliciting gimmicks as a platoon of dancing girls emerging from a pair of shoes, a giant baby carriage housing a dozen bawling babies, and a black-faced minstrel who suddenly turned white.

The story had something to do with Marjorie White recruiting all these generous stars to put on a benefit performance in aid of a minstrel show that is stranded along the Mississippi.

Yet to be heard from was Paramount, the fourth of the big studios of the time. In April of 1930, that company brought forth *Paramount On Parade,* on which a record eleven directors worked, under the supervision of Elsie Janis.

The cast included the already popular Maurice Chevalier, in three numbers, plus Clara Bow, Mitzi Green, Nino Martini, Nancy Carroll, George Bancroft, and many more. Two masters of ceremonies were not enough for this colossus, so it utilized three: Jack Oakie, Skeets Gallagher, and Leon Errol.

For comedy, there was a satire on Fu Manchu, with Warner Oland in that role, plus Clive Brook playing Sherlock Holmes, William Powell as Philo Vance, and Oakie as the victim of a murder.

Clara Bow danced with a group of sailors, Ruth Chatterton played a French girl looking for her missing marine, Nancy Carroll came out of a shoe, and the band accompanying her appeared in the shoe box. Chevalier's big number involved a small army of chorus girls forming a human rainbow. And little Mitzi Green did impressions of some of the other stars of *Paramount on Parade.*

It was much later that Arthur Mayer, a motion-picture sage, would say that an All-Star cast was a No-Star cast, the implication being that the presence of a dozen or more stars in a movie was only an indication of lack of faith (by the studio) in the individual box-office appeal of any of those stars. Mayer was right when he said it in the 1950s. By then, television had put such a dent in movie theater receipts that no All-Star cast could guarantee success. But in the early days of sound movies, audiences were dazzled by these opulent, star-studded Hollywood revues that capitalized on the public's taste for both stars and "inside" glimpses of movie magic.

At any rate, the Fox studio was happy enough with the success of its *Movietone Follies* to bring out a second edition, *The New Movietone Follies of 1930.*

This new edition was not quite as star-laden as other films of the time, but it had the popular comedian El Brendel in the lead, plus Marjorie

Paramount on Parade. Jack Oakie, Leon Errol, and Skeets Gallagher were all masters of ceremonies in this musical. (Paramount, 1930)

Paramount on Parade. Maurice Chevalier sang about sitting on top of a rainbow and sweeping the clouds away. Notice the human rainbow behind him. (Paramount, 1930)

New Movietone Follies of 1930. Miriam Seegar, El Brendel, and William Collier, Jr. were three of the principals in this musical comedy revue. (Fox, 1930)

White, William Collier, Jr., Frank Richardson, Noel Francis, J.M. Kerigan, and Miriam Seegar. There was less time and money spent on visual gimmickry in this one, more on jokes (He: "You told me I'm the cream in your coffee." She: "But you've turned sour.") and songs. Miss White paid tribute to the pipe dream that every young girl in the audience could identify with, in a song called "I'd Love to be a Talking Picture Queen."

But the Depression spreading across America was bound to affect the Hollywood studios, as well. For the next couple of years, the big splashy musicals were not quite as big or splashy. Warners came up with *Fifty Million Frenchmen,* with Olsen and Johnson, plus William Gaxton, John Halliday, and Helen Broderick.

Paramount switched its emphasis to radio, just then becoming a big, star-studded medium, and turned out *The Big Broadcast* (1932), with Bing Crosby, Burns and Allen, Kate Smith, the Mills Brothers, and the Boswell Sisters. (Paramount turned out several more Big Broadcast films in subsequent years.)

MGM gave us *Going Hollywood,* with Marion Davies and Bing Crosby, but more of the musicals of 1932-33 focussed on Broadway rather than Hollywood: *42nd Street, Broadway Through a Keyhole, Dancing Lady, Mr. Broadway,* and *Broadway Bad.*

In 1934, MGM tried again, rather half-heartedly, with a pastiche called *Hollywood Party,* which had Laurel and Hardy, Lupe Velez, Jimmy Durante, Charles Butterworth, Jack Pearl, and Ted Healey and his (Three) Stooges. But even with all these comics, plus a Walt Disney animated sequence, the picture failed to cause much excitement.

That same year, Fox came up with a big film that suggested awareness of the Depression, but also tried to serve as a tonic to ease the gloom.

Based on an idea by Will Rogers, it was first to be entitled *The Follies,* thus linking it with that studio's earlier successes. But it was changed to *Stand Up and Cheer.*

It concerned Warner Baxter as a theatrical producer hired by the president of the United States as Secretary of Amusements, with the specific assignment of putting on a show to cheer up the country. The "show" he put on — the bulk of the film — had such people in it as John Boles, comedians Mitchell and Durant, Sylvia Froos, Nick Foran, and Stepin Fetchit. *Stand Up and Cheer* also had a bonus — joining James Dunn and Patricia White in a song and dance number called "Baby Take a Bow" was an irresistible tyke named Shirley Temple. The movie was a rousing success — as was Shirley.

Altogether, Shirley made seven feature pictures

Hollywood Party. **Oliver Hardy, caught between two people who get him into fine messes: Lupe Velez and Stan Laurel. (MGM, 1934)**

Stand Up and Cheer. James Dunn and Shirley Temple, seen
here relaxing on the set, made audiences·stand up and cheer
with their song-and-dance routine. (Fox, 1934)

in 1934, in several of which she was teamed again with James Dunn, including one that took its title from the song Shirley sang in her first big film — *Baby Take a Bow.*

The musicals kept coming, but most of them now steered clear of plugging Hollywood, as if reminders of all that opulence in the midst of the Depression would be considered in bad taste. Paramount kept turning out its more or less annual Big Broadcast movies; Warners cashed in on their Gold Diggers series; MGM repeated their *Broadway Melody* success, adding a different year each time. RKO had Astaire and Rogers; 20th Century-Fox kept pushing Alice Faye, Warner Baxter, Jack Oakie, and Jack Haley. Even Universal got into the act with Edmund Lowe as *King Solomon of Broadway.*

Not until 1938 did the Hollywood musical about Hollywood make any comeback, and then only through two movies. The first was from Warner Brothers. Entitled *Hollywood Hotel,* it was a sort of double-header, combining the All-Star cast and studio glamor with the Cinderella theme, both before and since a staple of Hollywood films about Hollywood.

Among those playing themselves were Louella Parsons, Raymond Paige, and Jerry Cooper, all from the already established radio series of the same title, plus Benny Goodman and his orchestra.

Dick Powell played an ex-member of the Goodman band, stranded in Hollywood when his dreams of a screen test are dashed. And Rosemary Lane was a Hollywood hopeful who got her big break when she was "discovered" as a double for big, tempermental star Lola Lane. In time, Dick and Rosemary found each other, love, and success in the movies. And Johnny "Scat" Davis introduced the song that was to become a kind of symbol of the Hollywood Cinderella story — "Hooray for Hollywood."

Incidentally, the movie included the inevitable Hollywood premiere scene — with Dick accompanying Rosemary while thinking she was Lola — and the radio announcer covering the premiere was played by an unbilled young actor who had started in radio — Ronald Reagan.

The other 1938 film dealing with Hollywood was just as fanciful and perhaps somewhat more pretentious. It was *The Goldwyn Follies,* produced by Sam Goldwyn and released through United Artists.

Hollywood Hotel. Dick Powell and Rosemary Lane arrive at the big premiere with Louella Parsons. At right is Allyn Joslyn. (Warner Brothers, 1938)

The Goldwyn Follies. Seated are Kenny Baker and Andrea Leeds. Gathered around them: Helen Jepson, Phil Baker, Ella Logan, the Ritz Brothers, Bobby Clark, Vera Zorina, Charlie McCarthy, Edgar Bergen, and Adolphe Menjou. (United Artists, 1938)

Its cast included Adolphe Menjou, Vera Zorina, Andrea Leeds, Kenny Baker, Helen Jepson, Bobby Clark, Ella Logan, Edgar Bergen and Charlie McCarthy, the Ritz Brothers, and a ballet (for Zorina) choreographed by George Balanchine. It also had a score by George and Ira Gershwin and a script by Ben Hecht. Then, as always, Sam Goldwyn didn't fool around.

The story had Menjou as the producer of an upcoming movie, using young Miss Leeds as his gauge of public opinion. Miss Leeds "discovered" Kenny Baker, playing an unknown singer, and tricked Menjou into giving Baker his big break. In

The Youngest Profession. **Greer Garson gives her autograph to movie buffs Virginia Weidler and Jean Porter. (MGM, 1943)**

deference to Goldwyn's standing as a major producer, one critic described *The Goldwyn Follies* as "a superior hodge-podge."

The musicals continued, of course, for a good many years, but events led them into some different directions, as will be seen in later chapters. Films dealing with Hollywood (without music) also continued, but these too slipped into other categories to be covered later.

But the appeal of movies about Hollywood and its glamorous denizens continued to turn up from time to time. In 1943, for example, MGM released a "little" picture called *The Youngest Profession,* which dealt with the workings of a teenage movie fan club. Virginia Weidler and Jean Porter were the two energetic movie fans who haunted railway stations and hotel lobbies in hopes of cornering Hollywood celebrities for their autographs. But what carried the film was the roster of "guest" stars: Greer Garson, Lana Turner, Walter Pidgeon, Robert Taylor, and William Powell.

In 1947, Warner Brothers teamed two young players, Robert Hutton and Joyce Reynolds, in a lightweight comedy, *Always Together,* about a girl who inherits a million dollars but keeps it a secret from her boyfriend, a struggling writer, on the theory that the money will spoil him, a notion she picked up in the movies. In fact, Miss Reynolds is herself hooked on movies and, in the course of the film, imagines herself in various situations involving movie stars. The film accommodatingly dramatizes these daydreams, utilizing the services of a number of Warner Brothers stars: Errol Flynn, Humphrey Bogart, Jack Carson, Eleanor Parker, Dennis Morgan, Alexis Smith, and Janis Paige.

28

Always Together. Sudden heiress Joyce Reynolds gives a press conference. Seated next to her is Ernest Truex. (Warner Brothers, 1947)

Paramount had a slightly more substantial idea in 1947, in a star-heavy feature called *Variety Girl.* Based on the long history of philanthropy of the Variety Clubs (which began with the upbringing of a foundling girl abandoned in a movie house), the film had a fictional ward of the Variety Clubs, played by Mary Hatcher, landing in Hollywood and browsing around Paramount Studios.

Apart from the players involved in the story, the cast of celebrities encountered by Mary included virtually the whole Paramount roster: Bing Crosby, Bob Hope, Gary Cooper, Ray Milland, Alan Ladd, Barbara Stanwyck, Paulette Goddard, Dorothy Lamour, Sonny Tufts, Joan Caulfield, William Holden, Lizabeth Scott, Burt Lancaster, Robert Preston, Veronica Lake, William Bendix, Barry Fitzgerald, and such noted directors as Mitchell Leisen, Frank Butler, George Marshall, and that star among directors, C.B. DeMille.

Variety Girl. Roaming around the studio lot, Mary Hatcher meets many stars, including Gary Cooper. (Paramount, 1947)

Hollywood Barn Dance. Ernest Tubb, right, was the best known of the country and western singers in this musical. (Screen Guild Productions, 1947)

Hollywood Varieties. The Hoosier Hot Shots were among the vaudeville acts presented in this small budget effort. (Lippert, 1950)

From time to time, smaller studios or independent producers took a shot at cashing in on the Hollywood appeal, but usually with limited results. In 1947, for instance, there was *Hollywood Barn Dance,* which was simply a collection of country-western singers, including the then famous Ernest Tubb, doing their twanging best. And in 1950, there was *Hollywood Varieties,* with Robert Alda heading a cast of vaudeville acts strung together in a feature-length show.

But a couple of biggies still merit some mention. One was MGM's 1946 opus called *The Ziegfeld Follies.* (The same studio had already had considerable success with *The Great Ziegfeld,* in 1936, and *Ziegfeld Girl,* in 1941.) But this one shied away from any story line and concentrated instead on superior variety entertainment. It offered such goodies as Fred Astaire and Gene Kelly (in their only screen collaboration) doing a song-and-dance number entitled "The Babbitt and the Bromide;" a comedy sketch with Fanny Brice and Hume Cronyn; songs involving Lena Horne, Kathryn Grayson, and Astaire; and a witty production in which Judy Garland played a blasé movie star meeting the press.

In 1949, Warner Brothers coralled everyone on its lot to take part in *It's a Great Feeling,* in which Dennis Morgan and Jack Carson played themselves in a frothy story about Carson wanting to turn director. Among the stars who dutifully turned up were Gary Cooper, Edward G. Robinson, Joan Crawford, Danny Kaye, Jane Wyman, Sidney Greenstreet, Patricia Neal, and Eleanor Parker. In

It's a Great Feeling. Doris Day in a snit is enough to make Jack Carson cringe in this star-studded opus. (Warner Brothers, 1949)

addition, four Warners directors also appeared: Michael Curtiz, King Vidor, Raoul Walsh, and David Butler.

One reason these All-Star epics had begun to fizzle out by the end of the 1940s was that the studios, already beginning to feel the economic pinch of failing box-office receipts, plus the growing competition of television, had begun to prune their family trees. The days when the major studios could afford dozens of stars and scores of subordinate players, plus writers, directors, designers, and technicians on their staffs were drawing to a close.

More and more, actors and other hired hands were signed to short-term contracts, usually lasting

The Ziegfeld Follies. Judy Garland satirized a movie star's press conference in this production number. (MGM, 1946)

only for the shooting time of a specific movie. This made economic sense of course, but it also made it impractical to load a bunch of "guest stars" into a movie. Whereas in the past such stars were under contract and could be ordered to appear, however briefly, in one of the studio's star-studded extravaganzas, now it would be necessary to go out and hire them specifically for such assignments, and that would mean more money than the studios could any longer afford to pay.

The star-studded movie emphasizing the glamor of Hollywood was only one type of movie-about-movies. It was to get another good shot in the arm during the Second World War (chapter 6) when the unity required by the country's citizens seemed to call for a similar unity from Hollywood.

But the movies' interest in capitalizing on the public's fascination with Hollywood had many other strings to its bow. Over the several decades since movies became America's leading form of popular entertainment, there were to be hundreds of movies that dealt, in one way or another, with Hollywood and its most famous industry.

2 Hollywood's Dream Machine

The American public, which has for so long enjoyed a kind of tolerant amusement of the pomp and extravagance surrounding foreign royalty, has been able to have its cake too, by inventing an American equivalent of fairy-tale princes and princesses — the movie star.

We have always thought it quaint and old-worldish to see dukes, duchesses, and heirs apparent gamboling through the society pages of newspapers, presiding over the changing of some guard or other, marrying cousins of thin but indubitably royal blood, waving condescendingly at throngs of peasants.

But we have made just as much fuss over and shown just as much interest in the romances, conquests, dazzling successes, and abject failures of our own homegrown Hollywood royalty. For all our devotion to democracy, Gable was "the king" — not the president — of movie stars.

American tradition absolutely rejects the notion of rule by a monarch, but that does not make us immune to the vicarious joys of watching wealthy, glamorous, bejeweled, and beautiful people living the kind of life we would like to, but never really expect to, attain.

In fact, we have a slight advantage in America. In other parts of the world, one has to be born of royal blood. Here, one can theoretically get a transfusion of it from the contract-signing pen of a movie mogul or giant talent agency. According to the best traditions of the American dream, anyone can achieve our version of royal status — in Hollywood.

One of the most persistent myths about Hollywood has always been the idea that it is accessible to the lowly born, that anyone with enough talent, good looks, persistence, and a bit of luck could "make it" in the movies. And it is a myth that comes true just often enough to keep perpetuating itself.

Several generations of Americans have spent their lives believing that any nice, wholesome girl with a thirty-seven-inch bust could sit sipping a soda in Schwabb's and sooner or later be discovered. And who can count the number of chorus boys, life guards, collar ad models, and student actors who have dreamed of being right up there with Gable, Bogart, or Robert Redford?

That the Hollywood studios have done their fair share to keep this myth afloat is incontrovertible.

There was hardly ever a big musical in which the temperamental star did not sprain her ankle on opening night, thus affording her unassuming understudy a chance at stardom. Movies both silly and serious, dealing with Hollywood, have long relied on the basics of the Cinderella story. And millions upon millions of moviegoers lapped it all up happily and kept going back for more.

Even when Hollywood was kidding, it wasn't really kidding; even when movies treated the Cinderella story with some degree of tongue in cheek, the result was the same — Cinderella, or Cinderfella, won out against impossible odds and became a star, a new member of America's royalty. After all, if it happened to real people who went to Hollywood — and, from time to time, it did — then it could happen to people in movies and be no less believable.

An early example was a 1921 Ben Turpin movie called *A Small Town Idol*. Turpin, a veteran of the Mack Sennett shop, played a man engaged to his small town girl. He is falsely accused of a theft and forced to flee. He goes to Hollywood, substitutes for an actor in making a dangerous leap for the cameras, and becomes a star overnight. Later, he goes home to be acclaimed, but instead he is arrested for that old theft. Eventually, his girl-friend's father confesses that he framed Turpin, and all ends happily.

The same year, Will Rogers, already a big star via the Ziegfeld Follies on Broadway and in earlier silent films, had a romp in a feature called *Doubling For Romeo*. Rogers played Slim, a cowpoke reduced to "doubling" for various Hollywood actors in dangerous stunts. At one point, he dozes off while reading Shakespeare (!) and dreams he has to double for Romeo in a film of the Shakespeare classic. The visualization of the balcony scene (with Sylvia Breamer as Juliet) was a delight for Rogers fans — all the plain folk across America for whom the equally plain Rogers was a surrogate Romeo.

In *Mary of the Movies* (1923), Marion Mack went to Hollywood to earn money to support her family. After being forced to accept work as a waitress, she was spotted by some producer who decided she looked just like an ailing star and — presto! — fame and fortune followed. To add to the glamor, there were guest stars like Barbara La Marr, Estelle Taylor, Bessie Love, Louise Fazenda, and Rex Ingram.

Miss Brewster's Millions (1926) was a sex switch on an already well-known story. Bebe Daniels, as Polly Brewster, was a penniless Hollywood extra who inherited a million dollars (always a nice, round number, you'll notice) provided she could invest it successfully. An unscrupulous uncle (Ford Sterling) offers her five million dollars if she can spend her one million in thirty days. She has a ball doing this, only to learn that the uncle is penniless. But her investment in a movie company pays off and she and her young lawyer friend (Warner Baxter) find happiness and wealth.

Polly was a popular name for movie heroines of those days. There was *Polly of the Circus, Polly of the Follies, Polly of the Storm Country,* and *Polly with a Past*. And, naturally, there was a *Polly of the Movies*. This Polly (played by Gertrude Short) was an Arkansas girl who went to Hollywood to crash the movies. Her boyfriend invested $25,000 in the film she was in, but it looked as if it was destined to be a flop. However, a happy ending was stumbled over; intended as a melodrama, Polly's movie turned out to be a comedy instead, and a successful one. A wry comment, incidentally, on the efficacy of Hollywood.

Combining Hollywood pipe dreams with historical mystery was a 1928 movie called *Clothes Make the Woman*. Walter Pidgeon played a Hollywood actor who had been in Russia when the

Doubling for Romeo. **Will Rogers and Sylvia Breamer in their own version of Shakespeare's balcony scene. (Goldwyn, 1921)**

Married in Hollywood. Norma Terris and Douglas Gilmore in a scene from this early musical, full of dream sequences and other movie magic. (Fox, 1929)

Czar's family was murdered. But Pidgeon insisted he had helped Princess Anastasia to escape. Now, he wants to make a movie about the story, but has no ending. As if on cue, a pretty young Hollywood extra appears and . . . yes! . . . it's the mysterious Anastasia herself. Pidgeon proceeds with his movie, during the making of which someone tries again to kill Anastasia, but she survives.

Even more fanciful was *Married in Hollywood* (1929) with Norma Terris and J. Harold Murray. Based on an Oscar Strauss operetta, this one had Miss Terris as a Ruritanian princess. She and her prince (Murray) alternate between having spats and singing duets. Somewhere in the film, Miss Terris entertains at a ship's concert, where she is spotted by a film producer (Walter Catlett) who invites her to come to Hollywood, thus providing the film with its in-studio finale. Why the princess would not have told a Hollywood producer to stuff it is

Let's Go Places. Walter Catlett, in hat and glasses, was the big director in this inside-a-studio comedy. (Fox, 1930)

34

never explored. Miss Terris had been a big hit as Magnolia in "Showboat" on Broadway, and this seemed like a fitting vehicle for her screen debut.

Walter Catlett, a seasoned Hollywood comedy actor, played a film director in *Let's Go Places* (1930), which concerned itself with a young singer changing his name to something more glamorous in order to crash the movies. The deception worked, of course, even if the movie did not.

Show Girl in Hollywood (1930) had Blanche Sweet as a jaded film star (at one point she sang "There's a Tear for Every Smile in Hollywood"), and Jack Mulhall and Alice White as a couple of kids with dreams of Hollywood careers. There is a

Show Girl in Hollywood. Jack Mulhall and Alice White had an on-again-off-again romance in this comedy. (Warner Brothers, 1930)

Hollywood Speaks. Genevieve Tobin does her screen test, flanked by her mentor (Pat O'Brien) and her nemesis (Lucien Prival). (Columbia, 1932)

good deal of intra-industry chicanery before the romantic leads conquer Hollywood and our hearts, more or less in that order.

The innocent in Hollywood became a lasting stock figure. In *Playthings of Hollywood* (1931) there were three of them — Phyllis Barrington, Rita LeRoy, and Sheila Manners — sisters, this time, trying to crash the movies, and getting involved in all sorts of mayhem and melodrama.

Hollywood Speaks (1932) offered Genevieve Tobin as a girl dreaming of seeing her footprints in front of Grauman's Chinese Theater. She enlisted the aid of Pat O'Brien, a glib newspaper reporter, who succeeded in getting her a screen test and then a part in a movie being made by a lecherous director (Lucien Prival). This unpleasant experience was enough to make Genevieve give up her budding screen career and marry the reporter.

One of the more successful Cinderella stories of the time was *Going Hollywood* (1933) with Marion Davies and Bing Crosby. Miss Davies was approaching the twilight of her screen career, but Crosby was just on the way up. In the film, he played a popular crooner on his way to Hollywood with temperamental film star Fifi D'Orsay to work in a movie. They are pursued by Marion, as a smitten school teacher with a crush on Crosby. In time she replaces D'Orsay both in Bing's heart and in the movie being made. *Going Hollywood* had some good songs (including one of Crosby's biggest hits of the time, "Temptation") and a strong supporting cast that boasted Patsy Kelly, Stuart Erwin, and Ned Sparks.

The same year brought us *Sitting Pretty*, which had Jack Oakie and Jack Haley as a song-writing team bound for Hollywood. Along the way they meet Ginger Rogers, who helps put over their songs, plus assorted eccentrics like Gregory Ratoff, Thelma Todd, and Lew Cody. This was one of the first of what was eventually to become a long string of movies about Tin Pan Alley cats crashing the movies.

Alice Faye was a movie-struck girl from Peoria in *365 Nights in Hollywood* (1934), teamed with James Dunn as a former movie director who succeeds in making Alice a star. When he was not occupied with shaping Alice's career, Dunn ran a seedy little academy of dramatic arts for moppets.

The Countess of Monte Cristo, also in 1934, had Fay Wray and Patsy Kelly as a couple of movie extras who pose as a countess and her maid, on the

Going Hollywood. Marion Davies (standing) is just in time to save besotted Bing Crosby from the clutches of Fifi D'Orsay. (MGM, 1933)

perfectly reasonable theory that they could thus attract far more attention and carve out successful film careers. The cast also had Paul Lukas and Reginald Owen, who turned out to be as phoney as the countess and her maid.

Back in 1929, Harriet Lake appeared in the cast of *The Show of Shows,* although she was not among the seventy-five players who received screen credit. Her career went nowhere for a few years, but in 1933 she changed her name to Ann Sothern and began her movie work anew. In 1934 she was starred opposite Edmund Lowe in a little Columbia musical comedy called *Let's Fall in Love,* and Miss Sothern was on her way. In the film, Lowe played a director who is looking for a replacement for the temperamental star of his upcoming movie. She was

Sitting Pretty. Jack Oakie, above, was half of a song-writing team, and Ginger Rogers helped him and Jack Haley gain recognition in Hollywood. (Paramount, 1933)

supposed to be Swedish, so Ann pretended to be Swedish and got the part — and Lowe.

By now, Hollywood had pretty well implanted the belief in the public's mind that anybody could attain Hollywood stardom, with the right combination of initiative, gall, looks, luck and, maybe, a smidgen of talent.

Extras could pose as countesses to crash the movies; girls from Peoria could become stars; show girls could pretend to be exotic Swedes; school teachers could follow their idols to Hollywood and replace temperamental leading ladies; even mysterious Russian nobles could turn up in West Coast studios just in time to play mysterious Russian nobles.

There were yet more improbable switches coming. In 1934, James Cagney, already a star as the tough guy who shoved half a grapefruit into Mae Clarke's face, was presented in *Lady Killer,* in which he was first an usher, then a hood, and finally a movie extra — all in the same role. Mae Clarke was with him again, apparently ready and willing to suffer further indignities at the hands of lady-killer Cagney.

Still more bizarre was *Another Face* (1935), which had Brian Donlevy as an ugly gangster who has his face lifted to avoid detection. Having thus been outwardly metamorphosed, he gets it into his head that he is now good looking enough to become a movie star. Sure enough, he is discovered by Hollywood, and it is only the super-sleuthing of studio press agent Wallace Ford that finally unmasks Donlevy.

Another part of the Hollywood Dream Machine concentrated on yet a different approach — the klutz in Hollywood, a kind of lovable bull in an imitation china shop.

An early example in talking pictures was *Free*

365 Nights in Hollywood. **Frank Mitchell, Alice Faye, Grant Mitchell, James Dunn, and John Qualen facing a mob of potential movie moppets. (Fox, 1934)**

The Countess of Monte Cristo. Fay Wray (above with Paul Page) was the phoney countess, trying to crash the movies. (Universal, 1934)

Lady Killer. Russell Hopton, Raymond Hatton, Leslie Fenton, and Mae Clark, all under the spell of James Cagney, who muscled his way into the movies. (Warner Brothers, 1934)

Let's Fall in Love. Ann Sothern and Edmund Lowe, as actress and director, did just what the title called for. (Columbia, 1934)

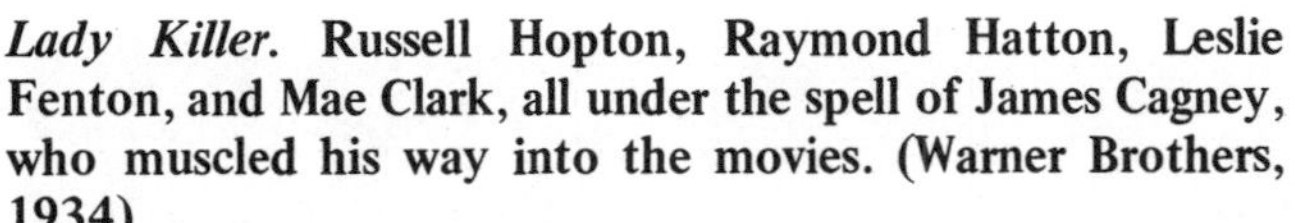

Another Face. That was what gangster Brian Donlevy got and it landed him in the movies, but Wallace Ford (right) was onto him (RKO, 1935)

Free and Easy. Not even Ed Brophy can believe that get-up on Buster Keaton. This was Keaton's first talkie. (MGM, 1930)

and Easy, which also happened to be Buster Keaton's first sound movie. This was in 1930, and Keaton had long been a silent screen favorite; critics and audiences were pleased to discover that Keaton's nasal voice did not hurt his comedy talent one bit. Keaton played a Kansas garage owner who accompanies his girlfriend to Hollywood when she is chosen "Miss Gopher City." Typically, the girl does not succeed in Hollywood, but Buster does. Most of the comedy was based on Keaton's bumbling around the studio, knocking over expensive equipment and otherwise driving the Hollywood types to distraction. To add some authentic atmosphere, the cast included three directors: Lionel Barrymore (who directed as well as acted in those days), Fred Niblo, and of course, Cecil B. DeMille.

The klutz in Hollywood framework was used to double advantage by a couple of later teams of comics. Olsen and Johnson brought their Broadway success, *Helzapoppin,* to the screen in 1941, and what it amounted to — besides the use of many typically zany sight gags — was an argument between Olsen and Johnson and their studio over how to make a movie of *Helzapoppin.*

In 1945, they did a variation on the same theme. This was *See My Lawyer* and it concerned Olsen and Johnson's attempts to break a movie contract. Once again, they worked in a string of sight gags, but this movie was not as well received as their earlier *Helzapoppin,* possibly because it did not have the value of a well-known title, as had their earlier venture.

The same year (1945) Abbott and Costello, by then a far more popular screen team, were seen in *Abbott and Costello in Hollywood,* a good example of the klutz in Hollywood. Bud and Lou were Hollywood barbers in one of those shops where all the manicurists dream of screen tests. After a series of unlikely events, they end up managing a young crooner who has been edged out of his movie career by a jealous rival. But the best fun came when Costello, hiding from studio police, gets trapped into being used as a dummy in a Western fight scene, tossed about by Mike Mazurki but unable to complain for fear of being exposed as an interloper. Again, for a touch of glamor, Lucille Ball, Preston Foster, and Rags Ragland appeared as themselves.

(There were more examples of the klutz in Hollywood, many of which are covered in other chapters.)

Another enduring Hollywood myth — only a slight variation on the Cinderella theme — was the notion that just plain folks, even as you and I, could take a trip to Hollywood and, if not crash the movies, at least rub elbows with some celebrities, who usually turned out to be just plain folks, too.

Among the plain folks who hit Hollywood were the Cohens and Kellys, two feuding families who had previously tackled (in movies) Atlantic City, Paris, Scotland, and even Africa.

In 1932 it was *The Cohens and Kellys in Hollywood,* with George Sidney (Cohen) and Charles Murray (Kelly) carrying on their inane

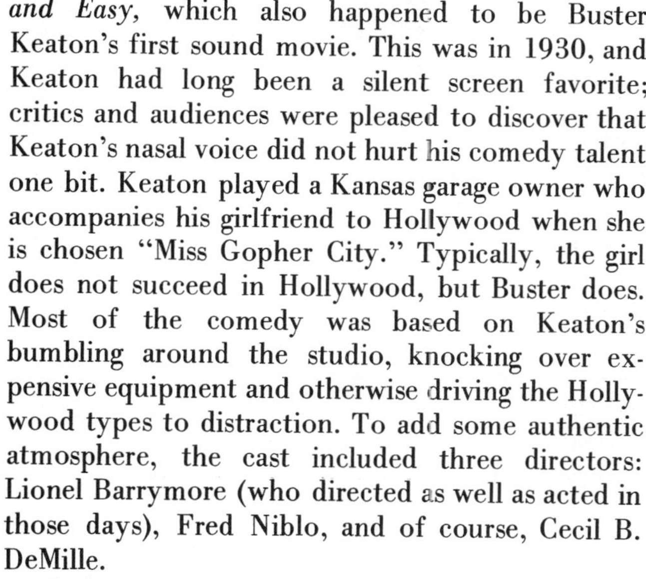

Helzapoppin. Chic Johnson and Ole Olsen are confronted by an irate Martha Raye in this famous revue brought to the screen. (Universal, 1941)

See My Lawyer. This time Olsen and Johnson wanted to break their movie contract. The trio around them are Alan Curtis, Noah Beery, Jr., and Richard Benedict. (Universal, 1945)

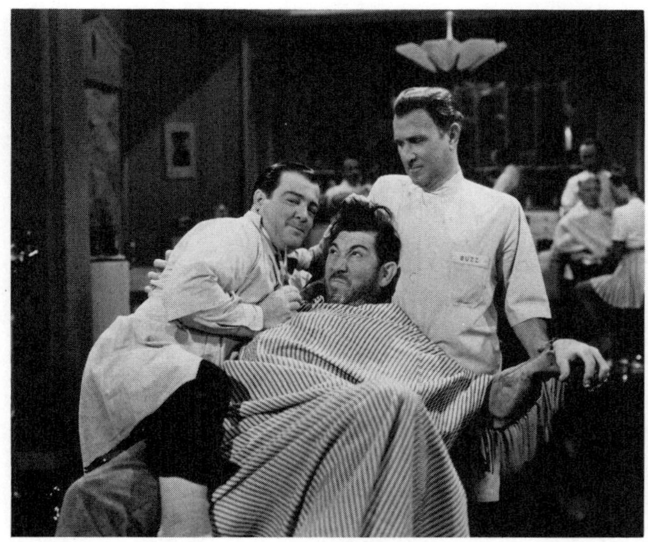

Abbott and Costello in Hollywood. That's Rags Ragland about to be shaved by Lou as Bud looks on. (MGM, 1945)

That's Right You're Wrong. Kay Kyser, flanked by Dennis O'Keefe and Ginny Simms, arrives in Hollywood. That's Roscoe Karns at right, and just behind him is Harry Babbitt. (RKO, 1939)

bickering against film studio backdrops. This time Kitty Kelly (June Clyde) got a movie role and her family quickly moved west. But the Cohens were not far behind, trying to outdo their rivals in "going Hollywood."

Kay Kyser, at the peak of his popularity in 1939, did a movie called *That's Right, You're Wrong* — a catch phrase from his "College of Musical Knowledge" radio series. The story involved Kay and his band, including Harry Babbitt, Ginny Simms, and Ish Kabibble, going to Hollywood to make a movie. But they cannot, because the assigned writers (Edward Everett Horton and Hobart Cavanaugh) cannot come up with a script.

Also in 1939, the Jones Family went to Holly-

The Cohens and Kellys in Hollywood. George Sidney and Charlie Murray were the title characters, and that's Eileen Percy with the camera. (Universal, 1932)

wood. Jed Prouty and Spring Byington were Pa and Ma Jones in this B-picture series that Fox threw together to compete with MGM's Hardy Family. The Joneses made some seventeen films in four years, dashing off to Paris vacations, visiting the racetrack, dabbling in business, and ultimately, having a fling at the movies. Like all their other lightweight adventures, this one only served to prove that revered American homily — there's no place like home.

Henry Aldrich, that popular American hero/klutz who started in radio, then went on stage and later struggled through a string of B pictures, got his crack at Hollywood, too. This was in 1943, in *Henry Aldrich Gets Glamor,* with Jimmy Lydon as Henry (he made some eight Aldrich films), winning a magazine contest and going to Hollywood as his prize. There he meets Frances Gifford, "the Sarong Queen," has his picture taken kissing her, and goes home a hero. But then, to back up his boasting, he must persuade her to visit his hometown. If you think he did not, you do not know your Henry Aldrich.

Tom Breneman was a well-known radio personality of the 1940s, with his program called "Breakfast in Hollywood." In 1946, a movie based on the series was released to practically no acclaim. The plot allowed Breneman to assist a budding romance between Bonita Granville and Eddie Ryan, had Zasu Pitts determined to win one of Breneman's contests for outlandish hats, and offered such extraneous goodies as the Nat King Cole Trio, the

The Jones Family in Hollywood. Jed Prouty and Spring Byington led their brood to Tinseltown and survived. (20th Century-Fox, 1939)

Henry Aldrich Gets Glamour. Jimmy Lydon was Henry, and Frances Gifford represented glamour as the "sarong queen." (Paramount, 1943)

Breakfast in Hollywood. Tom Breneman, the noted hat fetishist, is taken with the number on top of Zasu Pitts. (United Artists, 1946)

The Gashouse Kids in Hollywood. Milton Parsons, hands in ears, doesn't enjoy being serenaded by the Gashouse bunch. (Producers Releasing Corp., 1947)

Spike Jones band, singer Andy Russell, and Hollywood columnist (and mad hat devotee) Hedda Hopper.

The anybody-can-go-to-Hollywood theme may have stooped to its lowest level in 1947, with *The Gashouse Kids in Hollywood*. In this quickie, Carl (Alfalfa) Switzer and his buddies are all supposedly members of a Michael Whalen fan club, driving to the coast to meet their idol. On the way, they pick up a wierdo who is carrying a dead body in a coffin, and they later become embroiled in — and ultimately solve — a murder mystery.

Yet another switch of the Hollywood Dream Machine was the notion that Hollywood could come to you — or, at least, that part of it could. In the heyday of the movies, it was not unknown for

Go West, Young Man. Even though he wasn't too young, Warren William went for Mae West. (Paramount, 1936)

Hollywood personalities to make personal appearance tours, so the theme of stars seeing America and rubbing elbows with commoners was used for film plots.

One of the more amusing of these was *Go West, Young Man,* starring Mae West as a movie star on a personal appearance tour. Accompanying her was Warren William, as her press agent, mostly concerned with rescuing the star from any entanglements with wayside Lotharios. In the end, of course, her heart goes to the press agent. Among those she dallied with were Randolph Scott and Lyle Talbot.

Another way Hollywood stars could mingle with the populace was by going to college. At least, that is what Charles Starrett did in *Start Cheering* (1937), accompanied by his dim-witted press agent, Jimmy Durante. Predictably, he meets much

resentment on the campus, but everything works out in the end. And along the way, Columbia sprinkled such added attractions as singer Gertrude Niesen and the orchestras of both Johnny Green and Louis Prima.

The visiting movie star and the college campus were combined in 1943 in the film version of a bright Broadway musical hit called *Best Foot Forward.* Tommy Dix played the military school cadet who was brazen enough to ask Lucille Ball (playing herself) to be his date at the school dance. She accepted and turned up with her press agent (William Gaxton) for what turned out to be a lively and complicated visit. The results, however, were sheer fun, considerably enhanced by the presence of Nancy Walker, June Allyson, Chill Wills, and even Harry James and his Music Makers.

There was a time when the Western movie was

Start Cheering. **Jimmy Durante separates bully Broderick Crawford from movie star Charles Starret. (Columbia, 1938)**

Best Foot Forward. Lucille Ball was the film star, lured to the military school by cadet Tommy Dix. At right is William Gaxton. (MGM, 1943)

taken too seriously to provide the basis for any Hollywood-type story. But even that changed by the mid-1930s.

The same Charles Starrett who went to college in *Start Cheering* was the star of many B Westerns in the 1930s and 1940s. In one of these, *Cowboy Star* (1936), he played the title role, that of an actor in Westerns who got all dressed up in a tuxedo and allowed himself to be ogled by pretty girls — a distinct departure from the tradition that cowboy heroes loved only their horses.

In *Hollywood Cowboy* (1937), George O'Brien was the title character in a tale about a movie company making a Western on location. The interference of labor racketeers forces O'Brien to play a real-life cowboy to clear up the mess so the movie can be completed on schedule.

The Big Show, a Republic film of 1937, had

Cowboy Star. That's lantern-jawed Charles Starrett surrounded by female fans and Si Jenks trying to read the fine print. (Columbia, 1936)

Hollywood Cowboy. George O'Brien played the title role, Cecelia Parker was his girl friend. (RKO, 1937)

Hollywood Round-Up. Dicky Jones idolized stunt man Buck Jones (no relation) and helped him become a star. (Columbia, 1938)

The Thrill Hunter. Despite the business suit, Buck Jones (center) played a cowboy star, here waiting for the studio brass to respond to his latest demands. (Columbia, 1932)

Gene Autry in a double role: as Tom Ford, a Western star, and as Gene Autry, his double and stunt man. When Ford goes off on an unscheduled vacation, Autry has to pose as Ford to fulfill an appearance at the Texas Centennial. Autry is a big hit (he can sing, Ford can't) and when the hoax is exposed Autry gets a movie contract, then hires Ford as his double and stand-in.

Notice how the romantic old Hollywood myth of the understudy zooming to overnight stardom by filling in for the star on opening night was adapted to these Westerns about Hollywood.

In 1938, Buck Jones starred in *Hollywood Round-Up,* in which he was a double and stunt man for temperamental cowboy star Grant Withers. The jealous Withers tries to frame Jones to discredit him, but Helen Twelvetrees, who loves Buck, and her young brother (Dickie Jones) who worships him, help clear the good name of Jones. (Buck Jones had played a cowboy movie star earlier in *Thrill Hunter,* made by Columbia in 1932.)

Shooting High (1940) had what would seem like a pretty strong star combination — Gene Autry and Jane Withers. This one had to do with a movie company on location to make a movie about "Wild Bill" Carson, the town's first marshall. When Jane manages to dispatch the star (Robert Lowery) on a phoney mission, Autry, as a descendant of Wild Bill's, is hired to replace him. While a bank robbery is being filmed for the movie, it develops that the men doing it are not actors but real bank robbers, so naturally, Gene has to capture them all.

And so it went. *Bells of Rosarita* (1945) had Roy Rogers playing himself, on location making a Western and meeting Dale Evans (N O T playing herself), a sweet young thing beset by villains trying to swindle her. Roy rounds up other cowboy stars (Wild Bill Elliott, Allan Lane, Donald Barry) to put on a benefit show as a means of raising money to save Dale's father's ranch. Eventually, Roy and his "guest stars" even have to round up villain Grant Withers and his gang.

And in *Out California Way* (1946) Monte Hale, a cowpoke, crashed the movies with the aid of young Bobby Blake and the latter's horse, Pardner. But a jealous star (John Dehner) tries to foil Monte's career. In the end Monte wins it all — movie stardom, little Bobby's pretty sister (Adrian Booth), and his name in wet cement in the usual Hollywood location.

Shooting High. Gene Autry (on horse) and Jane Withers, next to him, were the co-stars. The romance was supplied by Marjorie Weaver, next to Jane. (20th Century-Fox, 1940)

In *Sons of Adventure*, a 1948 Republic Western, newly hired stuntman Russ Hayden was framed into accidentally killing the star of a movie in progress, when real bullets were put into Hayden's gun instead of blanks.

Meanwhile, back in the mainstream, the Hollywood Dream Machine kept working, turning out a seemingly endless parade of movieland myths, some more brazen than others in contriving variations on the theme.

Talent Scout (1937) had Donald Woods crossing the country, beating the bushes for promising young talent. He found Jeanne Madden, who was lovely and could sing, and, in time, they decided it must be love.

Ali Baba Goes to Town (1937) was an engaging musical vehicle for Eddie Cantor, in which he was

Sons of Adventure. Russ Hayden (in black outfit) has just accidentally killed the star. That's George Chandler examining the body. (Republic, 1948)

Talent Scout. Donald Woods was the potential star maker, and Jeanne Madden was one of those he tried to make. (Warner Brothers, 1937)

Ali Baba Goes to Town. Alan Dinehart, playing a director, is asked for an autograph by Eddie Cantor. (20th Century-Fox, 1937)

abetted by an impressive cast including Tony Martin, Roland Young, June Lang, John Carradine, Alan Dinehart, and Douglas Dumbrille. Cantor played a movie-struck autograph hound who was stranded in a desert and hired as an extra by a movie company on location. The movie soon drifted into a dream sequence in which Ali Baba (Cantor) applies New Deal techniques to the Baghdad of the tenth century, taking a few good-natured swipes at some of Franklin Roosevelt's policies, which were then regarded as controversial.

Less imaginative was *Pick a Star,* a minor 1937 effort from MGM, which had Resina Lawrence as an Iowa girl trying to crash Hollywood, Jack Haley as the nice guy who helps her, Mischa Auer as a ham actor, and Patsy Kelly as the heroine's sidekick.

Crashing Hollywood (1938) was even more mundane. Lee Tracy played a writer who, with the help of an underworld friend, got a studio writing job and then turned the tables on his former gangster cronies to expose them via film. Joan Woodbury supplied the heart interest, and the wasted cast included Jack Carson, Bradley Page, Lee Patrick, and Richard Lane.

In 1939, Sonja Henie and Tyrone Power were starred in *Second Fiddle,* which started out as if it were going to be a satire on the long search for the right girl to play Scarlett O'Hara, but didn't quite make it. The plot dealt with the search for the right girl to star in "Girl of the North" and she (Miss Henie) was found teaching school in

Crashing Hollywood. Screen writer Lee Tracy is on the carpet. At left are Jack Carson and Bradley Page. (RKO, 1938)

Second Fiddle. Movie hopeful Sonja Henie gives press agent Tyrone Power an affectionate tap, as Edna Mae Oliver looks on, icily. (20th Century-Fox, 1939)

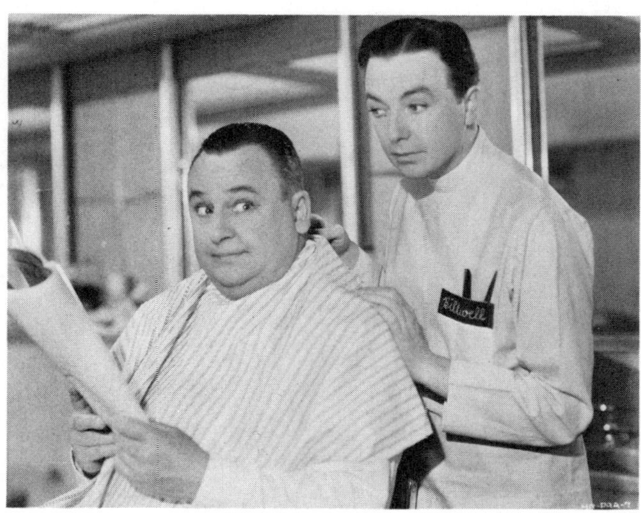

Pick a Star. Bert Roach gets trimmed by Jack Haley in a Hollywood barber shop. (MGM, 1937)

Minnesota. Plot aside, the film provided an excuse for Sonja to display her skill on ice skates, and a few Irving Berlin songs were tossed in for insurance. But the mixture was bland, at best.

Star Dust, released in 1940, was straight Cinderella-in-Hollywood. Linda Darnell started as a worker in a college town coffee shop, where talent scout Roland Young spotted her and whisked her off to Hollywood. Despite a good screen test, Linda's career was stymied because a studio cad (Donald Meek) had a blonde favorite he wanted to help instead. But Linda's hard-boiled dramatic coach (Charlotte Greenwood) managed to sneak Linda's screen test into the newsreel at a big Hollywood premiere. Result: success, overnight

Star Dust. Mary Healy, Linda Darnell, Roland Young, and John Payne all await the word from the front office. (20th Century-Fox, 1940)

stardom, footprints at Grauman's, and the man she loved, John Payne, all came to Linda.

In *Hollywood and Vine* (1945) Wanda McKay was a would-be actress who met Jimmy Ellison, a writer newly arrived in Hollywood. Only she did not know he was a writer and got him a job as a soda jerk. Ellison's life was further complicated by Leon Belasco as a producer who practiced nepotism.

A better chunk of entertainment was *Anchors Aweigh* (1945), an MGM musical that starred Gene Kelly, Frank Sinatra, and Kathryn Grayson. The two men played sailors on leave in Hollywood who meet a struggling extra and set about the business of getting her an audition with Jose Iturbi. Sinatra and Kelly were both great, but Miss Grayson was like a mermaid in a desert. Unable either to sing with Sinatra or dance with Kelly, she stood about

Hollywood and Vine. Jimmy Ellison (in beard) looks on as Wanda McKay plays a love scene with a rival. (Producers Releasing Corp., 1945)

50

Anchors Aweigh. Kathryn Grayson rewards Gene Kelly for promising to get her a screen test. At left is Frank Sinatra. (MGM, 1945)

mostly, looking very unconvincing. It might be said she showed none of the promise that she later failed to live up to.

But despite some pleasing musical moments (including one inspired live-plus-animated dance with Kelly and a mouse), the plot had to resort to pure Cinderella tactics to reach for a resolution. After Kelly and Sinatra fail to get her in to see Iturbi, Grayson accidentally meets the impressario in the studio coffee shop and learns her promised audition was merely a sham. But Iturbi is, after all, a human being. In the very next scene, Grayson is doing a screen test, complete with costume, make-up, lighting, full symphony orchestra, cameras grinding, Iturbi playing, conducting and smiling, and a movie contract practically in her pocket. That's the Hollywood Dream Machine operating in high gear.

Claudette Colbert played a Hollywood-bound novelist in *Without Reservations* (1946). On the train she meets a marine captain (John Wayne, no less) who seems to her ideal for the leading role in the film version of her book. Their comic misadventures included getting kicked off the train for drunkenness and having to hitchhike to Hollywood. To bolster this flimsy story, the studio (RKO) tossed in guest appearances by Jack Benny and Louella Parsons.

Really reaching was *Down Missouri Way*, a 1946 opus with Martha O'Driscoll, William Wright, and John Carradine. Miss O'Driscoll played an agricultural college professor who had trained a pet donkey so expertly that a movie company on location decided to use the donkey in a film. If anything saved the movie from total disaster it was Carradine's flamboyant portrayal of a director.

In 1948, in what turned out to be her last Hollywood movie, Sonja Henie starred in a remake

51

Without Reservations. John Wayne was a marine captain and Claudette Colbert was the novelist determined to make him a star. (RKO, 1946)

of *The Countess of Monte Cristo,* first made fourteen years earlier with Fay Wray. This time, Sonja and Olga San Juan were two barmaids who got jobs as extras, then borrowed costumes and props to pose as the countess (Sonja) and her maid (Olga) to be "discovered."

Once More, My Darling was a 1949 concoction with Robert Montgomery as a movie star-turned-lawyer who is asked by the United States Army to woo young Ann Blyth in order to get some needed secrets from her. To his surprise — and practically nobody's amusement — Miss Blyth was more than willing to be wooed and won by the aging film star.

My Friend Irma Goes West (1950) owed its title to the success of an earlier film *(My Friend Irma),* which starred dumb blonde Marie Wilson in a spinoff of her radio series. But the first movie also served to introduce Martin and Lewis to the screen, and their success spurred the sequel. Actually, it

Down Missouri Way. Martha O'Driscoll strikes a pose for the photographer. At right are William Wright and John Carradine. (Producers Releasing Corp., 1946)

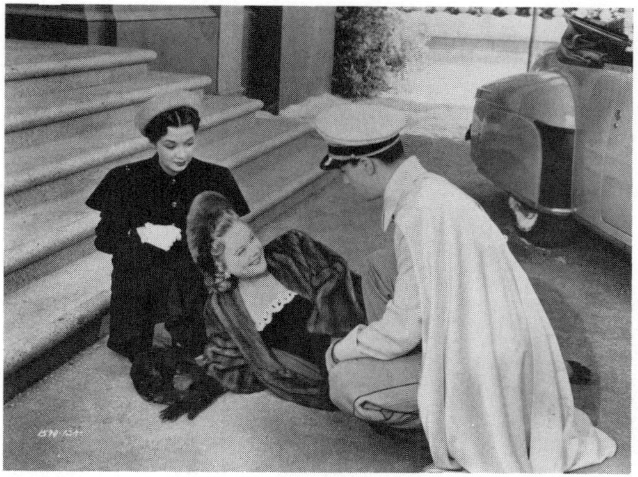

The Countess of Monte Cristo. What was good enough for Fay Wray was good enough for Sonja Henie fourteen years later. The "maid" at left is Olga San Juan. (U-I, 1948)

Once More, My Darling. The ex-movie star, Robert Montgomery, and his mother, Jane Cowl, share a martini and a few secrets. (U-I, 1949)

had less to do with Irma than with her friends, Dean and Jerry, heading West to break into the movies. John Lund, Corinne Calvet, and Diana Lynn were the other leading players.

Not only did Martin and Lewis do very well in Hollywood, both together and separately, but Lewis later made several films dealing with moviemaking, as will be shown presently.

In 1951, Ginger Rogers and Jack Carson were teamed in a dismal little comedy titled *The Groom Wore Spurs.* The groom was Carson and the reason he wore spurs was that he was a movie cowboy. Miss Rogers was a lawyer who married Carson and later had to defend him against a phoney murder charge.

Rainbow 'Round my Shoulder (1952) was a mildly entertaining musical, packaging the talents of Frankie Laine, Billy Daniels, and other pop performers of the time. The plot, what there was of it, involved Charlotte Austin and her budding movie career, with Arthur Franz as the man in her life.

Dick Powell, who had done the Cinderfella bit way back in 1936 in *Hollywood Hotel,* played a successful screen writer in *Susan Slept Here* (1954). Bent on writing about juvenile delinquency, he meets a homeless youngster (Debbie Reynolds) who is in trouble with the police. In no time at all, they are in love and married, despite the efforts of his former fiancée (Anne Francis) to break up the new romance.

The team of Dean Martin and Jerry Lewis split up in 1956, but not before the boys made yet another movie dealing with Hollywood. This was *Hollywood or Bust,* and it presented Dean as a reformed bookie and Jerry as a movie fan who decide to go West. Much of the picture deals with their comic journey, but Jerry finally meets his idol, Anita Eckberg, on a Paramount sound stage.

Hollywood's search for new ways to treat the Hollywood myth sometimes led to Broadway. One successful search resulted in *Silk Stockings* (1957). This hit Broadway musical by Cole Porter was a drastically revised version of the 1939 Ernst Lubitsch comedy, *Ninotchka.* In the original film, Greta Garbo was a Russian commissar in Paris, falling in love with the dashing Melvyn Douglas. *Silk Stockings* retained the "Ninotchka" character (played in the movie by Cyd Charisse) but switched the man to an American movie producer (Fred Astaire) in Paris to persuade a Soviet composer to write a couple of songs for him. Ninotchka was assigned to prevent this sellout to Western capitalism. To complete the triangle, there was Janis Paige as an American film star also interested in Astaire. The whole thing was a joyous romp, including a few musical jibes aimed at Hollywood mores.

Jerry Lewis, now working as a solo performer, turned his sights on Hollywood in *Rockabye Baby* (1958), even though the film was set in Indiana. Jerry's old friend, Marilyn Maxwell, is now a big movie star with a problem — triplets that the world does not know about. So Jerry is asked to serve as a foster parent for the infants temporarily. Although most of the movie concerns itself with

My Friend Irma Goes West. Jerry Lewis, Corinne Calvet, Dean Martin, and John Lund. Nowhere in sight is Irma, played by Marie Wilson. (Paramount, 1950)

Rainbow 'Round My Shoulder. Charlotte Austin, Frankie Laine, and Arthur Franz were in this Hollywood Cinderella yarn. (Columbia, 1952)

The Groom Wore Spurs. Jack Carson was a movie cowboy and his bride, Ginger Rogers, was a lawyer. (U-I, 1951)

Susan Slept Here. Dick Powell played an Oscar-winning writer in this comedy. (RKO, 1954)

Hollywood or Bust. Maxie Rosenbloom, Dean Martin, and Jerry Lewis. The bust remains unidentified. (Paramount, 1956)

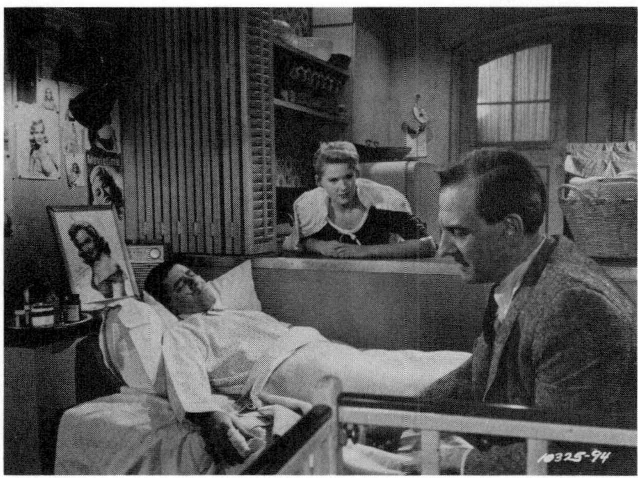

Rockabye Baby. Jerry Lewis, Connie Stevens, and Hans Conried got all mixed up in movie star Marilyn Maxwell's baby problems. (Paramount, 1958)

Silk Stockings. Fred Astaire and Cyd Charisse starred in this musical version of Ninotchka, which was given a Hollywood angle. (MGM, 1957)

Jerry's trials as a foster parent (and complications involving his girl friend, Connie Stevens, and her father, Baccaloni), *Rockabye Baby* also managed to poke a bit of fun at Hollywood-made religious spectacles.

A few years later, Lewis plunged into the category of the klutz in Hollywood. This was in one of his best comedies, *The Errand Boy* (1962), which had Jerry as a hapless bull in a Hollywood studio china shop. By now, Lewis had spent enough time around movie studios to be able to aim well his barbs at such Hollywood types as the assistant director (Dick Wesson) and the head of the mail room (Stanley Mann). Lewis co-wrote and directed *The Errand Boy,* and for insurance tossed in such Hollywood veterans as Brian Donlevy, Sig Ruman, Fritz Feld, Iris Adrian, and Doodles Weaver.

Lewis dealt with Hollywood once again in *The Patsy* (1964), in which he was a bellhop in a Beverly Hills hotel who was discovered by a desperate production company looking for a successor to their recently deceased star. It was the Hollywood Cinderfella theme again, tailored to the

The Errand Boy. Jerry Lewis did a lot of spoofing of Hollywood in this funny film. (Paramount, 1962)

special comic talents of Jerry Lewis — once again doubling as co-writer and director. In the cast were Everett Sloane, Keenan Wynn, Peter Lorre, Phil Harris, and John Carradine, again indicating Lewis's healthy respect for seasoned Hollywood supporting players.

Dear Brigitte (1965) was pure Hollywood hoke, with James Stewart as a folksy college professor whose young son (Billy Mumy) has a crush on Brigitte Bardot and virtually blackmails his father into taking him to France to meet the star of his dreams. It was, all things considered, not an especially memorable movie.

Even more depressing was *Harem Scarum* (1965), which was Elvis Presley's eighteenth feature film and probably neither better nor worse than some that preceded it. Presley played a Rudolph Valentino-type movie star who goes to the Middle East to promote his new film and ends

The Patsy. Jerry Lewis, again, as a klutz in Hollywood, required to record some songs. (Paramount, 1964)

Dear Brigitte. Ed Wynn, Glynis Johns, and James Stewart. Stewart's son had a crush on the lady of the title. (20th Century-Fox, 1965)

Boy, Did I Get a Wrong Number. Phyllis Diller, Bob Hope, and Elke Sommer all did, and so did the audience. (UA, 1966)

Harem Scarum. Elvis Presley, Jay Novello, and Billy Barty in a scene from this film-oriented musical. (MGM, 1965)

up being mixed up with all sorts of sheiks and other shady characters. Among those involved in this misdemeanor were Mary Ann Mobley, Fran Jeffries, Michael Ansara, and Jay Novello.

And to finish off what had clearly become a dry well, there was Bob Hope's tepid 1966 movie, *Boy, Did I Get a Wrong Number!* This had Elke Sommer as a movie star rebelling against her studio and hiding out in an Oregon bungalow rented by real estate man Bob. But even with Phyllis Diller tossed in as the standard comic family maid and Hope trying to keep Elke's presence a secret from his wife (Marjorie Lord), the movie went steadily downhill.

But however limp some of these later efforts at priming the Hollywood Dream Machine may have been, the movie about Hollywood and its residents was by no means finished. Fortunately, other directors, writers, and actors had taken different routes, explored Hollywood from different points of view, and found much entertainment still available.

3 Hollywood Kids Hollywood

Novels have kidded Hollywood. Broadway has kidded Hollywood. Radio and television have kidded Hollywood. And certainly newspapers and their critics have kidded Hollywood. All have done it in a variety of ways and with varying degrees of malevolence.

Hollywood's extravagance has been kidded; Hollywood's fakery, status symbols, nepotism, pomposity, heartlessness, phoney glamor, pretention, excesses, and insincerity all have been exposed to public view and ridicule.

But it is doubtful if any medium has done it more persistently and, sometimes, more incisively, than the screen itself.

The practice of poking fun at Hollywood began back in the days of the silent short. Often, the fun followed the successful release of some serious film.

For example, when Rudolph Valentino was all the rage as *The Sheik*, the Mack Sennett Studio released a broad takeoff on it with Ben Turpin, titled *The Shriek of Araby*. And when the same Valentino made *Blood and Sand*, it was Stan Laurel who saw its satiric possibilities and played a mock bullfighter in *Mud and Sand*.

Charlie Chaplin did a comic version of *Carmen*, in which he played a character named Darn Hosiery. And Will Rogers, having seen the success of *The Covered Wagon*, did a takeoff called *Two Wagons, Both Covered*.

Feature pictures, too, began to see the possibilities of kidding the already established Hollywood myths. In *The Extra Girl* (1924), Mabel Normand, one of the silent screen's most beloved comediennes, played a starry-eyed maiden bound to crash the movies. But the only movie job she could land was in the wardrobe department. The fun came when she was ordered to put a fake lion's head on a trained dog — because the studio lion

The Extra Girl. **Mabel Normand and Ralph Graves starred in this early Hollywood comedy. (1924)**

was not cooperating. Naturally, she got her animals mixed up and the real lion was dragged by her into the studio and proceeded to create comic havoc.

Probably the first classic of Hollywood-kidding was *Merton of the Movies,* made in 1924, with Glenn Hunter as the supreme klutz in Hollywood. The story had begun as a novel by Harry Leon Wilson, then was turned into a stage hit by George S. Kaufman and Marc Connelly, and the movie followed the play fairly closely.

Merton Gill, its hapless hero, takes a correspondence course in acting and spends much of his time daydreaming. The magnet of Hollywood draws him and he plunges earnestly into the business of becoming a serious actor. When he manages to get a job as an extra, a director begins to use him in the film, but without Merton's realization that he is being funny. Merton still has grand dreams until the opening night of the movie, when it finally dawns on him that he was not born to be a dashing, romantic hero, but a lowbrow comic actor.

Merton of the Movies was so successful that it was later remade twice, as well as serving as the unacknowledged model for many more films that combined kidding Hollywood with just enough pathos to touch off-guard audiences.

Before George Sidney became the Cohen of the Cohens and Kellys (with Charlie Murray as Kelly) he was teamed with Alexander Carr in a series of films in which Sidney played Abe Potash and Carr was Mawruss Perlmutter.

Potash and Perlmutter were scrapping business

In Hollywood with Potash and Perlmutter. Cyril Ring and Betty Blythe emote to opposite reactions from neo-moguls Alexander Carr and George Sidney. (Warner Brothers, 1924)

partners who survived various adventures, not the least of which was one titled *In Hollywood With Potash and Perlmutter* (1924). The two partners were movie producers here, and in addition to the old routine about thinking the lion was a dog with a lion's head on, there were some more original touches, including a sly dig at Hollywood nepotism, whereby Mrs. Potash ends up appearing in the first Potash-Perlmutter movie. Another good gag had the two neophyte producers interviewing Norma and Constance Talmadge for a role in their movie, but being good enough businessmen to pretend they have no idea who the famous sisters are.

Ella Cinders (1926) was a Colleen Moore vehicle, a cross between straight Cinderella and kidding the films. Ella goes to Hollywood on the strength of winning a photo contest (via a picture in which she looked cross-eyed due to a fly on the tip of her nose) and sneaks into a studio. A near-sighted director mistakes her for his star and puts her to work. There is the seemingly inevitable lion on the loose and Ella's terror at seeing it is mistaken by the director for deep grief over the loss of a baby, as called for in the scene he is shooting. To help live up to the title, there was even a Hollywood version of a wicked stepmother and a couple of ugly sisters.

Marion Davies starred in *Show People* in 1926 and helped turn it into a sizable hit, partly through

Merton of the Movies. Viola Dana and DeWitt Jennings. She falls for Merton, he gives Merton his movie break. (Paramount, 1924)

Ella Cinders. Colleen Moore, above, was the female equivalent of Merton in this movie-studio comedy. (Warner Brothers, 1926)

the tongue-in-cheek attitude of the movie itself, partly through Miss Davies' own willingness to poke a bit of fun at Hollywood and even herself.

She played Peggy Pepper, a Southern girl who crashes the movies and, after a certain amount of success, begins to take herself rather seriously. Blessed as she was with good connections (notably William Randolph Hearst), Miss Davies prevailed upon a number of top stars to do guest appearances, including Douglas Fairbanks, Charlie Chaplin, Karl Dane, Lew Cody, and Aileen Pringle. One of the gems of the film is the sight of Peggy Pepper deigning to give Charlie Chaplin her autograph, without recognizing him. Another has Miss Davies as Peggy seeing Marion Davies — as Marion Davies — and failing to be impressed by the star.

As for ribbing Hollywood techniques, there is a scene where a director commands Peggy to cry, but Peggy is unable to do so, thus jeopardizing a dramatic scene. The combination of off-camera mood music and the peeling of onions accomplishes the trick.

Perhaps less well-known but more delicious was a movie called *The Talk of Hollywood*, released in 1930, with Nat Carr and Fay Marbe as the stars.

In a way, it offered the most cynical view yet of both Hollywood and the public. Carr played a film producer who had endless problems, financial and otherwise, getting his movie completed. At the premiere, a drunken projectionist gets the reels mixed up and the resultant screening is a disaster. But wait! The bright young lawyer who is in love with Carr's daughter finds an unsuspecting distributor who buys the film as a brilliant burlesque — and it becomes a hit.

Show People. **William Haines and Marion Davies watch Marion on the screen, she with some apprehension. (MGM, 1928)**

Her Wedding Night (1930) was essentially one of those marital mix-up comedies, but the fact that the principals were supposed to be Hollywood folk helped make all the zaniness more likely. Clara Bow was a movie star trying to get away from it all; Ralph Forbes was a composer trying to get away from women; Skeets Gallagher was Forbes's chum, who agreed to pose as Forbes to draw off the females. Clara and Skeets got stranded at an inn on the Italian Riviera and, due in part to language difficulties with the proprietor, ended up married — only the papers showed Clara married to Forbes, because that is the name Skeets used. A few reels (and more yawns) later, she really did marry Forbes.

Two years later came *Make Me a Star*, the first remake of *Merton of the Movies*. With sound now

in use, the film was funnier than the original. This time around Stuart Erwin was the pathetic Merton, Joan Blondell was his worldly-wise girl friend, and veteran Ben Turpin was aboard for extra laughs.

Hot on its heels came *Movie Crazy* (1932) with Harold Lloyd playing a klutz somewhat akin to Merton. Lloyd gets a chance to act for the cameras and bungles everything. He repeatedly reaches for the telephone before it rings, for example. Lloyd also turns a formal dinner into a fiasco, offends the producer's wife, and otherwise makes himself a nuisance. But the producer (played by Robert McWade) is shrewd enough to recognize that Harold, without trying to be funny, makes people laugh, and so signs him to a contract.

Also in 1932, another Broadway smash hit lampooning Hollywood found its way to the screen. This was *Once In a Lifetime* by George S. Kaufman and Moss Hart, the production of which later provided Hart with the climax of his superb autobiographical book, "Act One."

Once again, the story was an exaggerated look at the madness of Hollywood, with particular emphasis on the view that incompetence and stupidity were no barriers to success. Jack Oakie and Aline MacMahon were prominent in the cast, which also included Zasu Pitts, Onslow Stevens, and Gregory Ratoff.

Next came *Bombshell* (1933) a diverting comedy with Jean Harlow as a blasé movie star and Lee Tracy as the publicity-hungry press agent. One of the plot twists had Harlow determined to adopt a baby and Tracy equally bound to stop her. To further his scheme, he dredges up Harlow's lowbrow father and brother (Frank Morgan and Ted Healey) to help make a bad impression on the adoption authorities. Also in the fine supporting cast were Franchot Tone, Pat O'Brien, Una Merkel, Ivan Lebedeff, and C. Aubrey Smith. But it was mostly the breezy, wise-cracking feud between Harlow and Tracy that carried the film.

Movies about movies had long since established the practice of depicting film directors (and sometimes producers) as eccentric, emotionally explosive, and sometimes evil characters, usually of undefined European origin. They strode around in jodhpurs, flailing riding crops, bellowing fractured English, making life miserable for poor, defenseless starlets and artistic writers alike. They were played, usually with great flair, by Gregory Ratoff, Leon Belasco, Lucien Prival, Luis Alberni, John

The Talk of Hollywood. Nat Carr and Fay Marbe were the stars of this wry comedy about moviemaking. (Sono Art-World Wide, 1930)

Her Wedding, Night. Skeets Gallagher and Clara Bow get married by mistake on the Italian Riviera. (Paramount, 1930)

Make Me a Star. **This remake of** _Merton of the Movies_ **had Stuart Erwin, right, in the title part. (Paramount, 1932)**

Movie Crazy. **Constance Cummings and Harold Lloyd, movie star and newcomer, respectively, in this comedy. (Paramount, 1932)**

Carradine, and other reliable character actors. (Ratoff, in fact, was as active in directing as in acting from the mid-1930s on). No doubt, these caricatures were based on Erich Von Stroheim, Michael Curtiz, and other European-born directors and/or producers who had invaded Hollywood from the earliest days of feature pictures.

Just such a full-blooded, flamboyant (but native-born) character was dreamed up by Ben Hecht and Charles MacArthur for their play, _Twentieth Century_, presented in 1932. Two years later, the film version was made, with Hecht and MacArthur doing the screenplay. The mad Broadway producer was splendidly played by John Barrymore, and Carole Lombard was the actress he would make a star.

On the stage, all the action took place aboard a train heading for New York, with the actress, by now a film star, encountering the producer, debt-ridden and desperate to lure her away from films and back to Broadway for his next production. But the film opened up the story, going back to the days when Barrymore browbeat a younger Lombard into giving a good performance in her first play. But much of the fun was still to be

65

Once in a Lifetime. This farce, based on a Kaufman-Hart play, had Jack Oakie and Aline MacMahon in leading roles. (Universal, 1932)

Bombshell. Jean Harlow was the mercurial movie star and Lee Tracy was her devious press agent. (MGM, 1933)

Twentieth Century. Carole Lombard's footwork gets to John Barrymore. She was a star, he a wheeler-dealer producer. (Columbia, 1934)

Bottoms Up. Spencer Tracy went to great lengths to make a star of Pat Patterson in this Hollywood send-up. (Fox, 1934)

found aboard that train, with the clash of these two massive egos, both irresistibly drawn portraits of theatrical eccentricity.

A film of somewhat less impact was *Bottoms Up* (1934) with Spencer Tracy as a fast-talking smoothie who turns his efforts to getting a movie career launched for Pat Patterson. Tracy, with sidekicks Herbert Mundin and Sid Silvers, boldly invades the Hollywood world of a comic producer (Harry Green) and his egotistical star (John Boles) and succeeds in passing off Miss Patterson as a British aristocrat, an identity that Hollywood bigwigs presumably cannot resist.

Ginger Rogers played a big movie star with a bit of an eccentricity in the 1934 comedy, *In Person.* Having been mobbed by her enthusiastic fans, she suffers an attack of agoraphobia and retreats to a hunting lodge where she meets George Brent who does not know who she is and, later, when he does,

In Person. Ginger Rogers was a runaway movie queen, but George Brent didn't know it. (RKO, 1935)

Stand-In. **Joan Blondell helped Leslie Howard bail out a movie studio in this bright comedy. (United Artists, 1937)**

proves unimpressed by her status. Naturally, this impresses her and in the end Ginger and George are in love.

Stand-In (1937) with Leslie Howard and Joan Blondell was a far more successful jab at Hollywood. Howard was an efficiency expert from New York sent to Hollywood by his bank employers to determine whether the film studio they own should be shut down. With the help of Blondell, a stand-in for glamorous star Marla Shelton, he finds that Marla and director Alan Mowbray are conspiring to destroy the studio by making Marla's upcoming jungle movie a flop. Howard unites studio employees and persuades them to keep the studio open long enough for producer Humphrey Bogart to re-edit the film and "save it" by cutting down Marla's footage and making the gorilla the star.

Carole Lombard was back at being a glamorous film star again in *Fools for Scandal,* a weak comedy that had Fernand Gravet playing a marquis who has no idea she is a star. They meet in Paris and since she does not know he is a marquis either, she hires him as her chef for her London home. In London, reporters discover that a French nobleman is living at film star Lombard's house, rival suitor Ralph Bellamy is appropriately shocked, and the whole mess ends with Lombard and Gravet in love.

By now, all sorts of glamorous movie stars were playing glamorous movie stars — or, rather, caricatures of them. In fact, RKO optimistically announced it would start a series of films (movie series were just getting to be all the rage then) about a movie actress named Annabel.

Lucille Ball was chosen to play Annabel, and Jack Oakie was her Svengali-like press agent. In the first outing, called *The Affairs of Annabel* (1938),

Fools for Scandal. Film star Carole Lombard hires a marquis, Fernand Gravet, as her cook, indicating that good help was as hard to come by as good plots. (Warner Brothers, 1938)

Annabel was to make a prison movie, so Oakie, striving for realism in her upcoming performance — plus a little publicity — has her committed to jail for a month for personal research. Later, he gets her a job as a maid, just because she is supposed to make a movie about a maid's life. Unpretentious and brightly written and acted, the series opener worked reasonably well.

The second film, titled *Annabel Takes a Tour,* came out only two months later. Again, Lucille Ball was Annabel and Jack Oakie was the fearless press agent assigned to keeping her name in the papers. The complications this time were a little less enjoyable, but the movie was well enough received that RKO would probably have continued the series had not Oakie demanded a hefty increase in salary. The economy-minded studio promptly

The Affairs of Annabel. Lucille Ball had the title part, that of a movie star, and Jack Oakie was her intrepid flack. (RKO, 1938)

Annabel Takes a Tour. Lucille Ball and Jack Oakie were also in this sequel, but the projected series stopped there. (RKO, 1938)

Boy Meets Girl. One of the cleverest of Hollywood spoofs, this had Marie Wilson and James Cagney (above), plus Pat O'Brien as Cagney's writing partner. (Warner Brothers, 1938)

called it off, thus terminating Annabel's career — though certainly not Lucille Ball's.

But 1938 brought us one of the brightest, broadest, and most memorable of zany satires on life in Hollywood. Once again, it came from the Broadway stage, but it suffered hardly at all in the transference to the screen.

The play was Sam and Bella Spewack's hilarious *Boy Meets Girl.* James Cagney and Pat O'Brien, by then well established as engaging foes on the screen, were the nutty screen-writing team responsible for turning Marie Wilson's baby (no longer illegitimate, as he was on the legitimate stage) into "America's Sweetest Sweetheart." Dick Foran was the totally square Western star who was the butt of many of the Cagney-O'Brien jokes, and Ralph Bellamy was the harried studio head who kept firing and rehiring them, depending on how desperately he needed them to straighten out the complications they usually caused. Among other things, the film gave Marie Wilson one of her best "dumb blonde" roles to date, and she parlayed that image into a lengthy career in years to come.

Although *The Bank Dick* (1940) was mostly a field day for W.C. Fields, it contained some broad jabs at Hollywood types. In it, Richard Purcell played a film producer on location in the town where Fields has just been hired as a bank guard. At one point, Purcell hires Fields to direct his film because the director (Jack Norton) is drunk. When Norton sobers up, Fields is back at being a bank guard, but he eventually foils an attempted bank robbery, picks up a reward, and is also paid

$10,000 for a screen story he sells to Purcell. One can readily see with how much respect Fields regarded the ruling heads of Hollywood.

A deliciously broad portrait of a Hollywood lamebrain was skillfully handled by John Barrymore in *World Premiere* (1941), a minor Paramount effort that yeilded more fun than anyone had a right to expect. Barrymore played a producer in the throes of planning a big Washington premiere for his wartime propaganda film, entitled "The Earth in Flames." By way of sabotaging his plans, the Axis send over three buffoons (Fritz Feld, Sig Ruman, and Luis Alberni) who succeed in substituting a German propaganda movie at the world premiere. It is one of the more wry touches of the film that producer Barrymore is not quite sure whether or not this is his movie that flashes on the screen. Also useful in the cast were Frances Farmer, Ricardo Cortez, Eugene Pallette, and others. But mostly it was Barrymore and the three mock foreign agents who provided the laughs.

Kiss The Boys Goodbye (1941) was taken from a play by Claire Boothe Luce that was a light satire on Hollywood's long and well publicized search for an actress to play Scarlett O'Hara. She invented a Southern belle named Cindy Lou who charmed her way into a big movie role. On the screen, Cindy Lou was played by Mary Martin, and Don Ameche was the director on the big talent hunt. But not much of Miss Boothe's barbed view of Hollywood was left. In its place was a light love story, some songs, and only a few limp jabs at Hollywood.

The Bank Dick. Ignoring the gunman at his back, W.C. Fields makes a deal with producer Richard Purcell for a movie story. (Universal, 1940)

Writer-director Preston Sturges, one of Hollywood's more original thinkers, turned his attention to the film medium and its messages in a cleverly conceived movie called *Sullivan's Travels* (1942). Joel McCrea, Sturges's protagonist, was a director of film comedies (rather like Sturges himself) who decided to make a serious "message" picture because the world situation was too gloomy to justify inconsequential comedy. To do research about "the real America," McCrea poses as a hobo and begins wandering across the land. But he later has trouble establishing his real identity and winds up in a convict camp, where he really learns how brutal life can be. Only then does he fully appreciate the importance of comedy entertainment in lightening the burden of those down-

World Premiere. John Barrymore, left, was the zany producer in this comedy. With him above are Frances Farmer, Ricardo Cortez, and Eugene Pallette. (Paramount, 1941)

Kiss the Boys Goodbye. Mary Martin used her Southern
wiles to charm movie director Don Ameche into a contract.
(Paramount, 1941)

Sullivan's Travels. **This first rate Preston Sturges film had Joel McCrea as a movie director in search of reality, but what he found was tough to take. (Paramount, 1942)**

trodden persons he had half envied. McCrea then returns to Hollywood, his respect for comedy renewed.

In the course of deflating some of Hollywood's more pretentious moviemakers, Sturges used the weapon of ridicule with sardonic ruthlessness — and he also succeeded in making a most entertaining "message" picture.

In a minor Republic film of 1942, *Yokel Boy*, Eddie Foy, Jr. played a "champion" moviegoer who was hired by a Hollywood studio as a barometer of public taste. Among his brilliant ideas was hiring a ruthless gangster (Albert Dekker) to play himself in a film the studio was basing on the gangster's life.

The Man Who Came to Dinner (1942) based on the hit Kaufman-Hart play, was not really about Hollywood at all, but its marvelous cast of characters included Lorraine Sheldon, well played by Ann Sheridan, one of those globe-trotting

Yokel Boy. **Eddie Foy, Jr. and Joan Davis were in this mild takeoff on a klutz in Hollywood. (Republic, 1942)**

actresses who juggle lovers and job offers with equal aplomb; Banjo, a Hollywood pixie modelled after Harpo Marx; and Beverly Carlton, who might as well have been called Noel Coward. All of them behaved as outrageously as Kaufman and Hart wanted us to believe Hollywood types do.

Rosalind Russell, who spent most of her years in films playing an endless procession of career women, was an authors' agent in *What a Woman* (1943). The author (Willard Parker) was a shy, bumbling college professor, and it was Miss Russell's task to lure him to Hollywood, where his novel was to be filmed. Somewhere along the way, she got the bright notion that he should even play the leading role in the movie. Once in Hollywood, Parker turned into a conceited wolf and it was up to Brian Aherne, as a journalist who had been tagging along making wry comments, to rescue Russell and claim her for himself.

The third film version of *Merton of the Movies* was made in 1947, as a vehicle for the comic talents of Red Skelton. The chief trouble with it was that in their zeal to make the movie suit Skelton, its makers lost much of the charm of the original story of Merton Gill. Still, it was rewarding for Skelton fans and included some gentle ribbing of early Hollywood.

Miss Tatlock's Millions (1948) with John Lund and Wanda Hendrix was about a Hollywood stunt man posing as the idiot member of a family trying to do a young lady out of her inheritance. Even with Barry Fitzgerald, Monty Woolley, and Richard Haydn in the cast, it came off like a script rejected by Jerry Lewis, mostly because Lund's impersonation of someone impersonating an idiot was woefully unfunny.

Don Ameche was a Hollywood director again in *Slightly French* (1949), with Dorothy Lamour more or less explaining the title. She was a carnival dancer with a flair for imitating various ethnic types, so Ameche, in trouble with his studio and his star, gets the bright idea of having Dottie pose as a glamorous French actress. Off they go to Hollywood to see their charade through. Love, as it must to all co-stars, eventually came to both the devious director and his posturing carnival dancer.

One thing Hollywood did well, from time to time, was to kid its own earlier days. A good example was *You're My Everything* (1949) with Dan Dailey and Anne Baxter as a couple of vaudevillians who landed in films at about the time

The Man Who Came to Dinner. Monty Woolley and Jimmy Durante are about to get rid of troublesome actress Ann Sheridan. (Warner Brothers, 1942)

What a Woman. Authors' agent Rosalind Russell created a monster in Willard Parker, left, but Brian Aherne was around to save her. (Columbia, 1943)

sound was coming in. The takeoffs of film styles of that time gave Miss Baxter a chance to do a flaming flapper bit a la Clara Bow. And there was a further development involving the film work of Dailey's and Baxter's daughter, played by Shari Robinson, which suggested the gooey sentimentalism of the Shirley Temple movies of the early 1930s.

Merton of the Movies. The third time around for Merton had Red Skelton as the hapless hero and Gloria Grahame as a Hollywood temptress. (MGM, 1947)

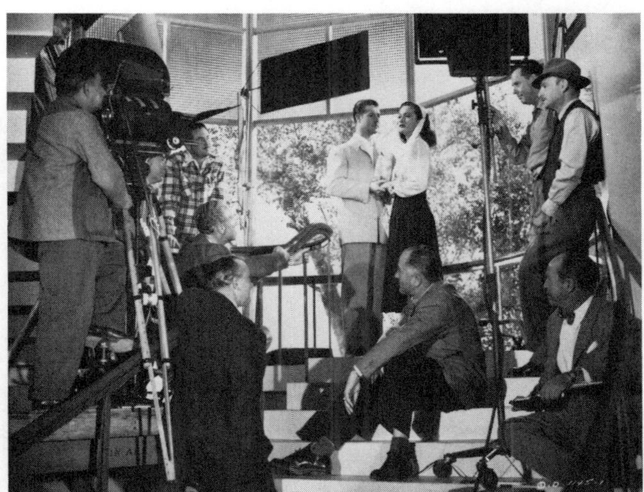

Miss Tatlock's Millions. John Lund plays crazy amid an assemblage including Richard Haydn, Monty Woolley, Wanda Hendrix, and Barry Fitzgerald. (Paramount, 1948)

Slightly French. Director Don Ameche tries to pass off Dorothy Lamour as a French actress. The film was slightly amusing. (Columbia, 1949)

You're My Everything. The director, Alan Mowbray, has to show Dan Dailey how to kiss Anne Baxter. (20th Century-Fox, 1949)

Even more fun was to be had with *Calloway Went Thataway* (1951), which had to do with the television success of the old films of a Western movie star, Smoky Calloway. In order to satisfy the demands of a huge audience of kids to see more of their "new" idol, a couple of advertising hucksters manage to dig up a double for him — a dumb Colorado cowpoke — and ship him off to Hollywood. Howard Keel played both the old Smoky Calloway (who turns up later in the film) and the innocent rube hired to impersonate him. Fred MacMurray and Dorothy McGuire were the hucksters, and Jesse White, Fay Roope, and Natalie Schafer rounded out the cast.

The following year brought one of the brightest examples of Hollywood satire on Hollywood yet, and surely one of the best movie musicals ever to come from Hollywood. It was the bubbling *Singin' in the Rain* (1952), with Gene Kelly, Debbie

Calloway Went Thataway. Fred MacMurray, Howard Keel, and Jesse White were all fine in this bright comedy about the re-emergence of an early cowboy star. (MGM, 1951)

Singin' in the Rain. **Possibly the best takeoff on early Hollywood, it had Millard Mitchell, Debbie Reynolds, Gene Kelly, and Donald O'Connor. (MGM, 1952)**

Reynolds, and Donald O'Connor as the engaging stars.

This one really had its fun at the expense of early Hollywood, when sound came along to threaten the careers of stars who could not adjust to the new requirements of filmmaking. Jean Hagen played (perfectly) such a star, a beauteous babe with a squeaky voice who was a star until the advent of sound threatened to expose her vocal inadequacy. Debbie Reynolds played the hopeful unknown who supplied Jean's singing voice, anonymously as far as the public was concerned, until Kelly and O'Connor found a way to destroy the temperamental Hagen and gain public acclaim for Debbie. In addition to some fine satiric swipes, the film also had some first-rate musical numbers that showed off the gifts of the stars.

Ben Hecht, an old hand at needling Hollywood while also taking its money, had some fun in the latter half of *Actors and Sin* (1952), a two-story package he devised. The first story, *Actor's Blood,* had to do with a retired actor's last bid for fame. But the second, called *Woman of Sin,* was a delicious little tale about a Hollywood agent (Eddie Albert) who discovers a steamy, sexy script, and pushes it toward major film production — only to find later that it was written by a nine-year-old girl, played in the film by Hecht's own daughter, Jenny Hecht.

Gloria Swanson, who had emerged from retirement so gloriously in *Sunset Boulevard* (chapter 5), tried it again with far less satisfying results in *3 For Bedroom C* (1952), a feeble comedy about a movie star (Swanson) crossing the country aboard a Hollywood-bound train with her college professor lover (James Warren) and a horde of hecklers trailing along.

A very amusing variation on the *Calloway Went Thataway* idea was *Dreamboat* (1952) with Clifton

Actors and Sin. Eddie Albert was the sharp Hollywood agent, Tracey Roberts his secretary, in this Ben Hecht double-header. This particular story was titled *Woman of Sin.* (United Artists, 1952)

3 For Bedroom C. Press agent Fred Clark has earned the wrath of movie queen Gloria Swanson in this tepid comedy. (Warner Brothers, 1952)

Dreamboat. Ginger Rogers and Clifton Webb, playing silent screen stars who meet again years later, were both good in this sly movie. (20th Century-Fox, 1952)

She's Back on Broadway. She was Virginia Mayo, a Hollywood type returning to the stage. With her above is Gene Nelson. (Warner Brothers, 1953)

Webb and Ginger Rogers. This time, Webb was a professor of English whose past comes back to haunt him: he had been a star of the silent cinema, one of those Valentino-type lovers, and his old movies are now being shown on television. Webb sets out to stop the further showing of his old movies and locks horns with huckster Fred Clark and his own old leading lady, Ginger Rogers.

Apart from needling, rather mercilessly, the ethics of television tycoons, *Dreamboat* generated much fun in its re-creation of the style of silent swashbuckling films, several samples of which are dropped into the movie, with Webb and Rogers hamming it up soundlessly in this series of manufactured "clips." And there was one hilarious scene in which Webb, annoyed by a barroom heckler, gets into a fight with the man, and tries, while watching his own old image on the bar's TV set, to duplicate the daring pugilistic feats he had managed back in his silent era glory.

Another valid theme was touched on in *She's Back on Broadway* (1953), with Virginia Mayo and Steve Cochran. Miss Mayo was the film star who returns to Broadway to give her shaky career a needed boost; Cochran was the Broadway director who loved her but feared she would just use his new show as a stepping-stone back to Hollywood. It was, at best, a minor musical comedy, but the basic idea was sound enough.

The actor's ego was superficially examined in *Kelly and Me* (1957), with Van Johnson as a vaudevillian who puts his dog into the act only to find that Hollywood thinks more of the dog than

the man. Also in the cast were Piper Laurie as the daughter of a film tycoon and Martha Hyer as a screen star.

A larger and less successful effort was *My Geisha* (1962), with Shirley MacLaine and Yves Montand. The latter played a film director blissfully unaware of the role his wife (Shirley) has played in his success. He goes off to Japan to make a movie of *Madame Butterfly* and Shirley masquerades as a geisha girl and lands the leading role in her husband's film — without being recognized by him. If this suggests that he could not have been a very perceptive husband, that was part of the idea. But, somehow, it did not seem all that convincing on screen, despite a noble effort by Miss MacLaine and some help by a cast that had Edward G. Robinson and Robert Cummings in it.

The V.I.P.s (1963) was a sort of Grand Hotel at the airport, with a group of characters whose lives are affected by the delay by fog of a scheduled airplane takeoff. The principals were Elizabeth Taylor and Richard Burton, but some of the lesser characters were more interesting. Among them was Orson Welles as one of those peripatetic film producers, just one step ahead of the bailiff. As an added touch this producer had a glamorous companion, played by Elsa Martinelli.

Island of Love (1963) also touched on moviemaking peripherally. Filmed in Greece, it dealt with a fast-talking operator (Robert Preston) being chased by a gangster (Walter Matthau) whose money he had spent on making a bad movie. The best thing in the film, apart from the scenery, was Matthau's offbeat portrait of a mobster.

Wives and Lovers (1963) was about a playwright (Van Johnson) who neglects his wife (Janet Leigh) so she pretends to have an affair with a movie star (Jeremy Slate) just to make him jealous.

No more distinctive was *Who's Been Sleeping in My Bed?* (1963) with Dean Martin as a television actor beset by the love-hungry wives of his pals. Even with Martin Balsam, Carol Burnett, Elizabeth Montgomery, and Richard Conte for support, it never got off the ground.

Mary, Mary (1963), based on a Jean Kerr play, also dragged in a Hollywood actor (played by Michael Rennie) as one of the participants in an innocuous marital comedy, with Debbie Reynolds and Barry Nelson as the bickering duo about to dissolve their gabby marriage.

William Holden played a harried screenwriter in

Kelly and Me. Vaudeville ham Van Johnson got to Hollywood, but it was his dog the producers really wanted. (U-I, 1957)

My Geisha. Yves Montand was so wrapped up in directing that he didn't even see through the disguise of his wife, Shirley MacLaine. (Paramount, 1962)

The V.I.P.s. Elsa Martinelli, Martin Miller, and Orson Welles were among the people stranded at London's airport. (MGM, 1963)

Island of Love. Robert Preston was a hustling moviemaker threatened by gangster Walter Matthau. At right is Tony Randall. (Warner Brothers, 1963)

Wives and Lovers. Janet Leigh and Van Johnson were shakily married, and the agile type above is Jeremy Slate, a movie actor Van suspected of fooling around with Janet. (Paramount, 1963)

Who's Been Sleeping in My Bed? Diane Foster, above with
Martin Balsam, was one of several wives pursuing Dean
Martin. Nobody really slept in anybody's bed, but a lot did
at the theaters. (Paramount, 1963)

Mary, Mary. Barry Nelson dozes off while his wife, Debbie Reynolds argues. At right, rear, is Michael Rennie, as an actor who tempted Debbie. (Warner Brothers, 1963)

Paris When it Sizzles. Screenwriter William Holden got help from Audrey Hepburn in finishing his story, but it hardly seemed worth it. (Paramount, 1964)

Paris When it Sizzles (1964), with Audrey Hepburn as his helpful secretary. Holden, living in Paris, is supposed to rap out a script in three days, and the movie tried desperately to be funny by having Holden and Hepburn act out various versions of the script they are wrestling with. But most of the comedy was flat, and even such stalwarts in the cast as Noel Coward and Tony Curtis did not help.

The Panic Button (1964) used Italy as its locale and involved the making of a TV movie specifically to lose money and save taxes for some underworld types. Maurice Chevalier played a washed-up actor hired for the film, Jayne Mansfield was to be his leading lady, Eleanor Parker was Chevalier's agent, and Michael Connor was the unhappy man charged with carrying out the unsavory mission. Oh, yes, the switch was that the resultant film ended up winning an award. But *The Panic Button* did not.

The underworld was dragged into filmmaking again in *After the Fox* (1966), a Peter Sellers comedy that missed its mark. Sellers was an escaped convict posing as a movie director in Italy,

The Panic Button. Eleanor Parker and Michael Connors were two of the principals in this yarn about a movie planned to be a flop. No comment. (Gorton, 1964)

Good Times. Sonny and Cher played themselves in this amusing daydream about how to make their first film. (Columbia, 1967)

After the Fox. Peter Sellers, above with Victor Mature, was an Italian criminal posing as a film director. (United Artists, 1966)

The Party. Peter Sellers turned a Hollywood party into a shambles in this labored comedy. With him above is Claudine Longet. (United Artists, 1968)

but really concerned with trying to get some stolen gold into the country. Victor Mature, Britt Ekland, Martin Balsam, and Akim Tamiroff were also in the cast. Saddest of all, the script was by Neil Simon and the movie was directed by Vittorio de Sica.

Sonny and Cher, at a time when they were a top pop recording duo, made a pleasant little movie called *Good Times* (1967), which dealt with Sonny and Cher, as themselves, being approached to make a movie and visualizing for us what might have happened if they had made it in various ways — as a Western, a crime thriller, a jungle adventure, etc. Probably because it did not pretend to be anything more than a light romp for its stars, it was reasonably rewarding.

Peter Sellers again aimed his sights at Hollywood in *The Party* (1968) and missed again. This was a Blake Edwards exercise in which Sellers played a stupid actor from India crashing a posh Hollywood party and turning it into a shambles. Despite Edwards's frantic efforts to put Sellers into all sorts of mad situations, it was not a notably enjoyable party, even with all the standard Hollywood types and props available.

The Secret Life of an American Wife (1968) had Anne Jackson as a suburban housewife who tries to pose as a $100 call girl in order to make the acquaintance of an irresistibly attractive movie actor. All this is prompted by the mistaken belief that her husband (Patrick O'Neal) no longer loves

84

The Secret Life of an American Wife. **Her secret was an affair with movie star Walter Matthau, but her husband, Patrick O'Neal, left, discovered it. (20th Century-Fox, 1968)**

her. But what saved the picture from failure was the inspired casting of rumpled, aging, unromantic Walter Matthau as the glamorous movie star.

In a strange sort of way, it was a return to Merton Gill, the original nonromantic image of a Hollywood star. Perhaps Hollywood's self-kidding had come full circle, poking fun again at the most ludicrous aspects of the glamorous image it has for so long both fostered and, in frequent schizoid departures, debunked.

In half a century or more of feature films, perhaps only a small fraction of Hollywood movies effectively poked fun at Hollywood. But in a world of industries so solemnly concerned with their own public image, precious few of them have shown that much self-awareness.

Hollywood movies have made fun of Hollywood venality, fakery, glamor, egocentricity, extravagance, and stupidity. There have been such high-water marks as *Boy Meets Girl, Sullivan's Travels, Calloway Went Thataway, Merton of the Movies, Twentieth Century, Stand-In, Dreamboat,* and *Singin' in the Rain.*

It can be argued that no other medium of popular entertainment — not theater nor radio nor the music business nor television — has shown as much initiative or candor in spoofing its own shortcomings.

4 Hollywood Shows its Heart

In movies dealing with the private lives of royal personages, the focus has often been on showing audiences that kings, queens, and their most intimate friends have hearts just like everybody else, laugh, cry, eat, love, suffer, and die, just as we ordinary mortals do. That's the way the public has always wanted it.

Since Hollywood's hierarchy represents the popular American equivalent of European royalty, it stands to reason that, from time to time, there should be Hollywood films in which stars, directors, producers, writers, and their respective spouses are shown to have hearts, to suffer setbacks, to love foolishly, even to make great sacrifices for the benefit of someone else.

Given the film industry's vast resources for any manner of propaganda, it is not unreasonable to expect that those resources should occasionally be put to use in patting film folk on the back.

This has been done, over the years, with varying degrees of success, sometimes shoddily, sometimes slickly, sometimes even with a convincing touch of sincerity. And, as with royal stories, that is what the public likes.

Some of these films, particularly in earlier days, were unabashed tear-jerkers, as soapy as *Madame X* or *Back Street* or *Stella Dallas,* except that they dealt with the slings and arrows attacking movie people.

Souls for Sale. **Note the violinist providing mood music so the young actress, Eleanor Boardman, can emote. The director, at right, was played by Richard Dix. (Samuel Goldwyn, 1923)**

An early example was *Souls for Sale* (1923) which, despite its provocative title, had little to do with the selling of any souls. It was about a girl with the quaint name of Remember Seddon, who jumped a Los Angeles-bound train because she was beginning to have second thoughts about her new bridegroom.

Where she happened to jump was a desert, where Remember fell asleep only to be awakened by an

Arab sheik talking English. The sheik was an actor with a film company on location. Remember soon fell in with these Hollywood people, learning, to her surprise, that they were just plain folks. Before long, she decided she wanted to be an actress too, and even managed to get a screen test. The results were so bad that she broke down and cried, whereupon the director told her that if she could cry like that on camera she might yet become a star.

The villain of the piece was Remember's husband, who turned up again just in time to supply a finale, of sorts. Wanted for murder, and jealous of the director who had befriended Remember, he ended up getting killed.

Remember Seddon was played by Eleanor Boardman, Richard Dix was the kindly, dedicated director, and Lew Cody was the evil husband. One critic headlined his review of *Souls for Sale* "Democratic Hollywood" and described it as "the first picture giving a very fair idea of motion picture life in Hollywood."

Even more indicative of the big heart that breathes within Hollywood was a 1924 feature entitled *Inez From Hollywood*, based on an Adela Rogers St. John story called "The Worst Woman in Hollywood."

The worst woman (Inez) was played by Anna Q. Nilsson as a high-living, giddy movie queen. But there was a secret and more humane side to Inez, for although her vast public knew nothing about it, she was supporting a poor sister in New York. In fact, even the poor sister did not know that her money was coming from the worst woman in Hollywood.

But Lewis Stone, an aging roué, tripped over this information and later, in New York, looked up sister Fay, played by a rather demure Mary Astor. When Inez hears there is hanky-panky going on between Stone and poor sister Fay, she hotfoots it to Gotham planning to shoot the cad. But she soon learns that her sister and the man are truly in love and she backs off.

One of the more poignant, if corny, movies of the genre was *The Legend of Hollywood* (1924), with Zasu Pitts and Percy Marmont in the leading roles.

Zasu was an aspiring actress and Percy a would-be writer, both hanging on for dear life in a Hollywood that was aloof to them. They were, of course, in love, but not at all in demand.

Inez from Hollywood. Lewis Stone falls in love with Mary Astor, Inez's sweet sister, and Inez has to like it. (Warner Brothers, 1924)

The Legend of Hollywood. One of those two remaining glasses of wine is poisoned, and Percy Marmont doesn't know which one. (PDC, 1924)

In desperation, Percy conceives an intriguing way of ending his troubles. Having mailed out his latest and presumably greatest script to the studios, he takes seven wine glasses and fills them. He also puts a dash of poison in one of the glasses, then mixes them up so he does not know which one contains the poisoned wine. He proceeds to drink one glass of wine per day, and this game of wino's roulette stretches to the seventh day — and the last (and presumably poisoned) glass.

When that day's mail still brings no favorable response from the studios, he drinks down the last glass of wine, fully prepared to die. Then, and only then, does he get a phone call telling him a studio chief is crazy about his script.

But dear, sweet, loving Zasu, wise to his suicide plot, has switched glasses again, removing the poison and supplying in its place a happy if implausible ending.

Broken Hearts of Hollywood (1926) was a variation on the *Madame X* theme, with a movie-land setting. Louise Dresser was the big movie star who turned her back on her family to devote her time to her career. But the obligations of mother-hood became apparent to her when her daughter, played by Patsy Ruth Miller, got mixed up with a no-good wolf. Louise dispatched the cad to save her daughter, but, as any good daughter would, Patsy Ruth took the stand at Mama's trial to plead for mercy for her.

Sometimes, the theme seemed to be that all the

Broken Hearts of Hollywood. **Patsy Ruth Miller, above, was Louise Dresser's devoted daughter in this tear-jerker. (Warner Brothers, 1926)**

The Runaway. **William Powell and Clara Bow were both movie types, devoted to each other, until she accidentally shot him. (Paramount, 1926)**

The Last Command. Evelyn Brent and Emil Jannings were the leads in this drama about a Russian general who ends up in Hollywood, playing a Russian general. (Paramount, 1928)

glamor and excitement of Hollywood stardom were not worth the price. This came through, if dimly, in *Broken Hearts of Hollywood.* It was somewhat more strongly stated in *The Runaway* (1926), with Clara Bow, Warner Baxter, and William Powell.

Clara was the film actress, ambitious in her career, who accidentally shoots William Powell while they are on a movie location in Tennessee. Because she cannot prove it was an accident, Clara becomes the runaway of the title and is sheltered by a kindly mountaineer, Warner Baxter.

To add a little melodrama, there is a mountain feud in process and George Bancroft, representing the opposing family, is on the verge of killing Baxter when who should turn up but William Powell, who was not dead after all. It is Powell who disposes of Bancroft and then wants Clara to return with him to filmland. But Clara has found true love with mountaineer Baxter and spurns the glitter and tinsel of Hollywood.

Emil Jannings, one of the most popular of silent film actors, made an unusual and generally successful film in 1928 called *The Last Command.* He was seen as a former general of Czarist Russia, now struggling along in Hollywood (one can only wonder why) until he is called to play the part of a Czarist general in a movie.

The extras in the film scoff at Jannings's tales of having been a general but we, the audience, know better, because we are shown flashbacks of his earlier and more colorful life. In fact, it develops that the man working as director of the film (William Powell) is also from Russia and had served under General Jannings. The far-reaching tentacles of coincidence get a good workout in *The Last Command,* what with a genuine White Russian general, temporarily a Hollywood extra, being cast to play a genuine White Russian general, and the director of the film having been an underling to the aforesaid general in Mother Russia and now putting Jannings through his paces in a Hollywood studio. Still, the movie was really a vehicle for the histrionics of Jannings and he did not let his fans down. In addition, the supposedly hard, cynical Hollywood types were shown to have some compassion for this exiled Russian militarist.

What Price Hollywood, in 1932, was a soapy melodrama about Constance Bennett's rise to stardom and her realization that fame and glamor are not everything in life. She starts out as a Brown Derby waitress, gets a break from director Lowell Sherman, is made a star by producer Gregory Ratoff, and marries playboy Neil Hamilton. But Hamilton tires of living in her shadow and leaves her, just before she bears his son. Next, the director, having turned drunkard, kills himself, and Constance gives up everything and flees to France. But Hamilton follows her and Constance at last finds true happiness, far from the madding close-up.

In 1933, MGM turned out one of those three-generation sagas of a family of entertainers, starting in small-time vaudeville and ending in Hollywood. Frank Morgan and Alice Brady were The Hacketts, who later changed their billing to The Three Hacketts, to include their son (played by Jackie Cooper as a boy, then by Russell Hardie as an adult). Partly because of the father's old-fashioned approach to entertainment and partly because of the son's ambitions, the act breaks up. When the son is drafted and sent overseas, never to return, the older Hacketts take care of their grandson — Mickey Rooney, at first, who grows up to be Eddie Quillan.

The grandson finally clicks in Hollywood, and Morgan and Miss Brady, his now elderly grandparents, go to live with him in a plush Beverly Hills mansion. Apart from the heartaches of career ups and downs, the film seemed to be saying that the generation gap existed even in show business, and that high living in Hollywood was not necessarily the key to enduring happiness.

What Price Hollywood. Constance Bennett acts for director
Lowell Sherman, but her heart wasn't in it. (RKO, 1932)

Broadway to Hollywood. Frank Morgan, Jackie Cooper,
and Alice Brady were a vaudeville family who eventually
went Hollywood. (MGM, 1933)

The Moon's Our Home. When Henry Fonda fell for Margaret Sullavan, he didn't know she was a movie star. (Paramount, 1936)

More frothy was *The Moon's Our Home* (1936), a comedy romance starring Margaret Sullavan and Henry Fonda. Basically, it was no different from all those Claudette Colbert-Fred MacMurray or Irene Dunne-Cary Grant romances in which love triumphs over common sense. But Sullavan was a high-spirited movie star and Fonda was a travel writer. Before meeting they each had formed rather low opinions of the other and when they did meet it was incognito. Of course, they fell in love, married and had a brief honeymoon before fate separated them. Then, they had the tricky task of finding each other again, though neither one knew the other's real identity. Pure fluff, of course, but reasonably good fun and, perhaps more important, it showed the beautiful people of the time experiencing real, honest-to-goodness emotions, just like everybody else.

It Happened in Hollywood (1937) was more authentically a Hollywood movie with heart, in that it dealt with a cowboy star of the silents (played by Richard Dix) who is persuaded to change his style with the coming of talkies. Forced into evening clothes and sophisticated roles, he flops, but still has enough respect for his fans that he refuses to play gangster parts. In time, his fans rally (led by moppet Billy Burrud) and Dix becomes a big star all over again.

The movie was an unpretentious B entry that might have fared better than it did, except for one thing: it was pointlessly compared with a movie released earlier in the same year, a movie that was to become something of a landmark in Hollywood stories with heart.

That deservedly famous film was *A Star is Born,* with Janet Gaynor as Esther Victoria Blodgett, one of those millions of hopefuls who trudge to Hollywood; and Fredric March as Norman Maine, a big star whose drinking and irresponsible behavior mark him as a man doomed to fall from grace.

They meet while Esther is working as a serving maid at a big Hollywood party and, before long, Maine is using his influence with studio-head Adolphe Menjou to get her a screen test.

We next see the emergence of Vicki Lester (even her name is glamorized) in one of those montages that depict her going through makeup, wardrobe, being coached on how to walk, how to act, etc. But a star is indeed born and even though Vicki and Norman are in love and dash off to be married, their troubles do not take too long closing in on them. Norman's career is in a tailspin as hers rockets upward, and both are powerless to alter the outcome.

After Norman Maine has disgraced himself and made life intolerable for Vicki, he finally takes himself out of her life by walking into the Pacific Ocean. And when, after all her grieving, she is forced to make a public appearance again, she reaffirms her love for her dead husband by the spunk of her self-introduction to the crowd — "This is Mrs. Norman Maine."

Miss Gaynor, at the tail end of her own long and successful screen career, turned in a sweetly moving performance as Esther Victoria Blodgett. And Fredric March, whose career still had a good many years to go, was superb as the well-meaning but weak Norman Maine.

In addition, the script was spiked with sardonic comments that lent it an air of candor. Producer Menjou, for instance, on the subject of the movie public: "Fans will write to anyone for a picture. It only takes a three-cent stamp and that makes pictures cheaper than wall paper." And Lionel Stander, as the tough studio publicity man who never liked Norman Maine, could not even temper his dislike when Maine was drowned: "First drink of water he's had in twenty years, and then he had to get it by accident. How do you wire congratulations to the Pacific Ocean?"

Seen again on television, after many years, parts of the movie seem overly sentimental and Miss Gaynor's emoting comes across as rather limp. But

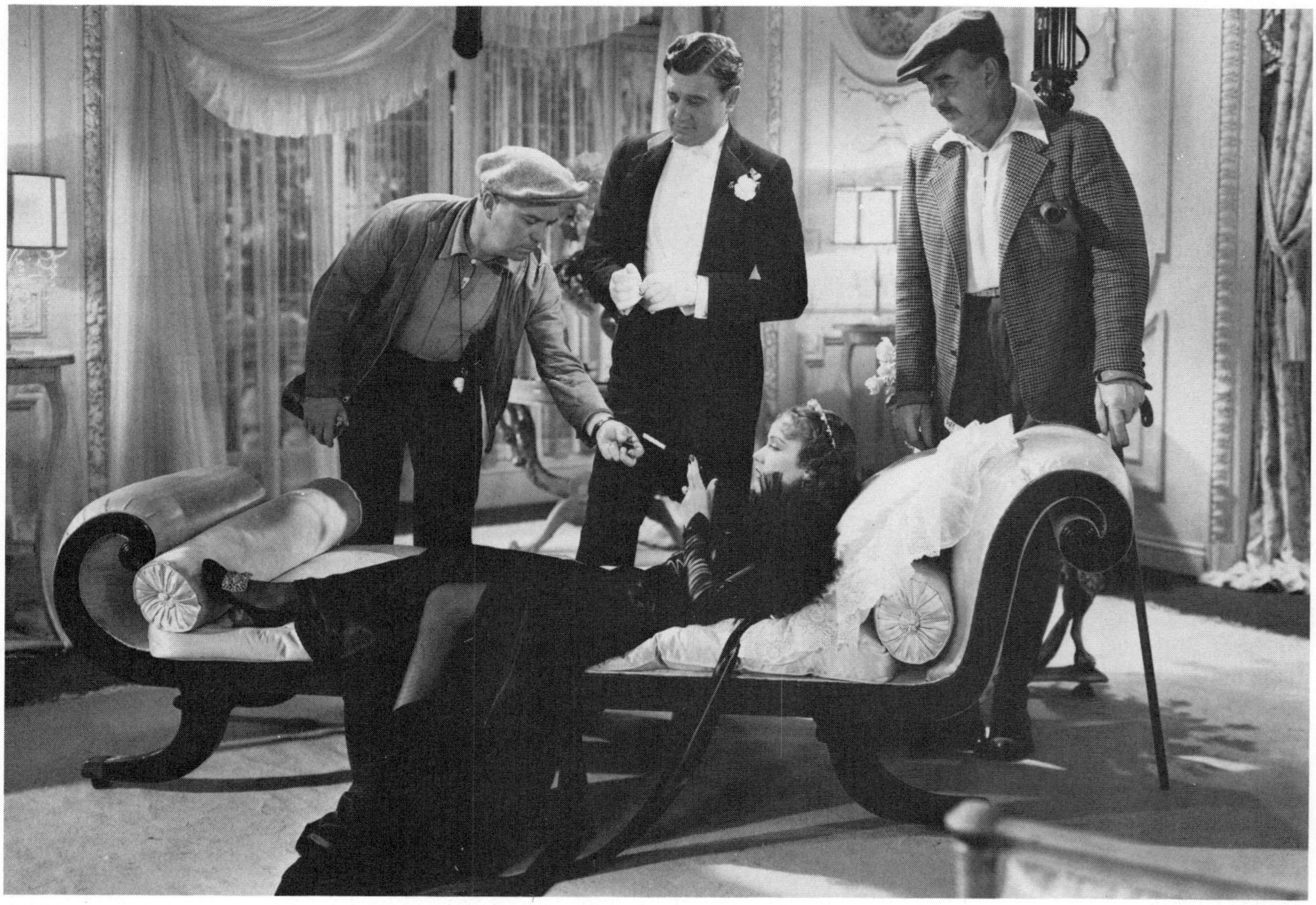

It Happened in Hollywood. Ex-cowboy star Richard Dix has to dress up and do a love scene with Fay Wray. (Columbia, 1937)

A Star Is Born. Janet Gaynor, Fredric March, Adolphe Menjou, Lionel Stander, and Vince Barnett. One of the best of the Hollywood heartbreakers. (United Artists, 1937)

the spice of the dialogue is still tasty, and the essentials of the tragic decline of a movie star past his prime can still be affecting.

A different view of the fall-and-rise aspect of a movie man's career was offered in *Hollywood Cavalcade* (1939) with Don Ameche and Alice Faye in the leading roles. Presumably because that year marked the fiftieth anniversary of American movies, this film tried to combine a sketchy history of the development of motion pictures with a dramatic story about some "typical" denizens of the film capital.

As did the later (and much better) *Singin' in the Rain, Hollywood Cavalcade* found some fun in ribbing the early days of movies and even in the transition to sound. Rounded up were a small platoon of silent screen comedians — Buster Keaton, Ben Turpin, Chester Conklin, Hank Mann, et al — to do Keystone Cops and custard pie-throwing bits. There was even Mack Sennett, playing himself.

But the drama somehow lacked the gripping quality of *A Star is Born*. Ameche was a movie pioneer, a director in the silent days whose imagination and resourcefulness supposedly helped advance the art of cinema. Miss Faye was both his leading lady and the light of his life, but she walked off and married Alan Curtis, which caused Ameche to go into a slump that did not end until he (a) realized the potential of the new talking pictures, and (b) got his girl back. Also in the cast were J. Edward Bromberg as a producer and Stuart Erwin as Ameche's loyal sidekick.

A more oblique approach to displaying the heart of Hollywood was the 1941 film, *Hold Back the Dawn,* with Charles Boyer, Olivia de Havilland, and Paulette Goddard. Actually, the Hollywood angle had little to do with the main body of the story but served, instead, to bookend the love and adventure tale.

Essentially, the story was about a homeless European ladies' man (Boyer) who romances and then marries an American school teacher (de Havilland) in a Mexican border town, simply as a means of gaining legal entry to the United States. On their honeymoon, he falls in love with her and risks all to avoid destroying her happiness.

But the film opened with Boyer striding into a Hollywood studio and offering to sell his story to a director, played by Mitchell Leisen, who, in fact, directed this movie. Boyer's story is then told in flashback, after which the intrepid United States Immigration official (Walter Abel) catches up with Boyer and hauls him off to the Mexican border again. However, there is a happy resolution, with Abel helping Boyer to re-enter the United States and be re-united with Miss de Havilland.

Only the most cynical observer might be tempted to question the likelihood that an alien on the run could simply march through the Paramount gates and into a sound studio, and then be lucky enough to encounter a man as courteous as Leisen, who apparently thought nothing of holding up his own filming while he listened to the sad tale of woe of a perfect stranger. How dare anyone imply that Hollywood had no heart!

Hollywood Cavalcade. **Stuart Erwin, Alice Faye, and Don Ameche were the leads in this drama of early Hollywood. (20th Century-Fox, 1939)**

Hold Back the Dawn. **Walter Abel puts the arm on Charles Boyer just as Boyer finishes telling his story to director Mitchell Leisen. (Paramount, 1941)**

Weekend at the Waldorf. **War correspondent Walter Pidgeon helps film star Ginger Rogers fight off the old ennui. (MGM, 1945)**

Weekend at the Waldorf (1945) was a reworking of the Grand Hotel theme, this time based at the famous New York hostelry and introducing an assortment of characters who are thrown briefly together under one elegant roof.

Of prime interest here was Ginger Rogers, who played a glamorous movie star who is, wouldn't you know, unhappy despite it all. It seems that in all of Hollywood she has been unable to find one man worthy of her heart. Then she meets Walter Pidgeon, the smooth, pipe-smoking war correspondent who is also staying at the Waldorf. After the usual ups and downs, their romance hits a familiar and happy plateau. But despite some breezy dialogue and such other distractions as Lana Turner, Van Johnson, Edward Arnold, and even Xavier Cugat and his orchestra, the Waldorf weekend seemed like a long one.

Miracle of the Bells (1948), based on a popular novel of the time, tried to tell of the death of a film actress and its effect on various people in her hometown. But it misfired, for the most part, and came out somewhere between straight soap opera and tasteless hinting at miraculous happenings.

Alida Valli (billed at the time merely as Valli) was the young actress from a mining town who becomes a big movie star, mostly through the efforts of press agent Fred MacMurray. But she dies after the completion of a movie and her body is shipped back to her hometown for burial. Press agent MacMurray lurks about sounding gloomy, and Frank Sinatra, as the local priest, tries to find a higher meaning to the glum goings-on. Then, when a shift in the local church's foundation causes a couple of religious statues to turn, this is whipped up into the appearance of a miracle — mostly by way of creating publicity for the dead girl's just-completed movie. All in all, the film was a clumsy attempt at showing that when the chips are down people — even Hollywood people — are not so bad, after all.

Then, there was *Dancing in the Dark* (1949) in which William Powell played a has-been actor who is hired by a movie studio to go to New York and sign up a certain musical comedy star to come to Hollywood for a big film. Instead, Powell "discovers" unknown Betsy Drake and brings her out to the studio.

Despite their initial shock, the studio moguls soon recognize that Miss Drake is, indeed, dazzlingly talented, and everything seems fine until she decides she does not want to do the picture. And why? Well, it turns out that the same Mr. Powell is really her father and, what's more, that he had deserted her mother way back sometime before the movie started.

The film included a number of musical spots — mostly from the Broadway show "The Bandwagon" — but neither they nor the contrived story could save the movie from the obscurity to which it was deservedly relegated.

In 1953, MGM issued what has turned out to be a fairly popular movie about Hollywood, shown frequently on television, admired both for its surface slickness and its underlying sentiment. *The Bad and The Beautiful* had a large cast of stars: Kirk Douglas, Lana Turner, Walter Pidgeon, Dick Powell, Gloria Grahame, Barry Sullivan, and Gilbert Roland.

At first glance it appeared to be one of those now-it-can-be-told exposés, about the ruthless producer (Douglas) who uses and misuses people to gain his own ends. He makes a star of Turner, then

Miracle of the Bells. Frank Sinatra, Lee J. Cobb, and Fred MacMurray were involved in this drama about a dead movie star being shipped home. (RKO, 1948)

Dancing in the Dark. William Powell, center, was a has-been actor who "discovered" a newcomer: his own daughter. (20th Century-Fox, 1949)

The Bad and The Beautiful. Barry Sullivan, Lana Turner, Dick Powell, and Walter Pidgeon met to talk about the film producer they all hated, and needed. (MGM, 1953)

dumps her when she falls for him; he mistreats director Sullivan; he lures a novelist (Powell) to Hollywood and dangles a gigolo (Roland) in front of Powell's bored wife (Grahame) so that Powell will be free to concentrate on his script.

All these vignettes are told in flashback, with studio head Pidgeon having assembled the principals in an effort to persuade them to once again work with the now discredited Douglas. But while appearing to cater to their egos, Pidgeon is subtly reminding them all that, whatever his brutal methods, Douglas had helped their careers. So, in the end, all agree to let bygones be forgotten and, typically, become dazzled by Douglas's latest project.

Despite its lack of depth, *The Bad and The Beautiful* still conveyed a kind of reality in capturing the surface grain of Hollywood life, and it certainly indicated that, whatever their failings, movie people were surely not heartless. The film's major failing was in the murkily drawn character played by Douglas; it never succeeded in getting inside him — or, perhaps the failure was Douglas's.

The following year came one of the most touching of all movies about Hollywood and that rarest of all films — a remake better than the original. This was the 1954 version of *A Star is Born,* with Judy Garland as Vicki Lester and James Mason as Norman Maine.

(There are those who regard this as the third version, citing the 1932 film, *What Price Hollywood,* as the original. But the similarities are tenuous, at best, and the quality of that early movie is far below that of its two successors.)

There were changes, of course, mostly to make proper use of Judy Garland's talents as a performer. Instead of haunting casting offices in search of film work, she was introduced as a vocalist with a small band, a girl content in her work, never dreaming she has the potential for greater stardom. It is Norman Maine who takes her, pushes her in and up, helps build her into a star, falls in love with her, and then goes to pieces himself.

The producer this time was played by Charles Bickford, with a touch more warmth and humanity than Menjou had suggested in the 1937 film. And Jack Carson played the cynical publicist every bit as well as Lionel Stander had done in the earlier version.

But several factors made this a superior film. First of these was Garland's performance. At the very top of her form, she was compelling in her handling of the songs and dances given her; one piece ("Born in a Trunk") remains a high-water mark in film musical production for its inventiveness and wry humor. Another factor was the way the musical numbers were woven into the movie's story, a rare enough sign of believable construction.

Mason was every bit as impressive as March had been, likable despite his excesses, pitiable in his inability to cope with the decline of his own career while his wife's continued upward.

But the film's greatest strength was Garland herself, even when she was not singing. Her

96

A Star Is Born. Charles Bickford, Judy Garland, James Mason, and Jack Carson were the principals in this fine remake of the Gaynor-March movie. (Warner Brothers, 1954)

dramatic performance had all the depth of emotion that Gaynor's missed. That air of vulnerability that seemed to hover around Garland's head from the time she first journeyed to Oz was never more useful nor more affecting.

Sad to relate, Miss Garland's own personal problems caused such havoc in the production of the film that much of Hollywood had lost patience with her, with the result that when Academy Award time came around what was judged was not her on-screen performance but her off-screen tantrums, and she missed the best chance she ever had for an Oscar. Nevertheless, she and all those associated with this splendid film gave us an ineradicable picture of Hollywood showing us its heart.

The same year brought us another engaging portrait of a tragic film figure in *The Barefoot Contessa* (1954), with Ava Gardner in the title role and Humphrey Bogart as the director who sparks her career.

The movie was set mostly in Europe, but there were Hollywood types involved. Besides Bogart, there was Warren Stevens as a ruthless producer and Edmund O'Brien as a weak but likable publicist.

The girl (Ava) is a gypsy dancer, discovered in Madrid and turned into a star. But it is her affairs with various men that the story concerns itself with mostly: first Stevens himself, whom she rejects, then Marius Goring, also spurned, and finally Rosanno Brazzi, as a count she falls in love with and marries, only to learn he is impotent.

The gloomy, moody film, written and directed by Joseph L. Mankiewicz, had some caustic comments to make on the nature of movie people, but Miss Gardner's acting range was somewhat more limited than the role demanded.

The Barefoot Contessa. Ava Gardner was the enigmatic gypsy girl who became a film goddess. (United Artists, 1954)

A few minor entries of the time are worthy of mention, too, if only because each tried to do its bit to show us a human side of Hollywood.

In 1954, for instance, there was *Hollywood Thrill Makers,* which dealt with the problems of movie stuntmen. William Henry played a film stuntman and James Gleason was his manager. Henry starts by telling his kids, via flashback, why he quit stunt work; then he comes out of retirement for one big job to aid his late buddy's widow.

Slim Carter (1957) was about a movie cowboy, played by Jock Mahoney, whose career was shaped by publicist Julie Adams. Success quickly goes to his head and he becomes an insufferable boor, until a boy (Tim Hovey) wins a contest and comes to spend a month at Slim Carter's home. In time, the innocent tyke brings out the best in Slim, who ends·up doing a dangerous movie stunt (even

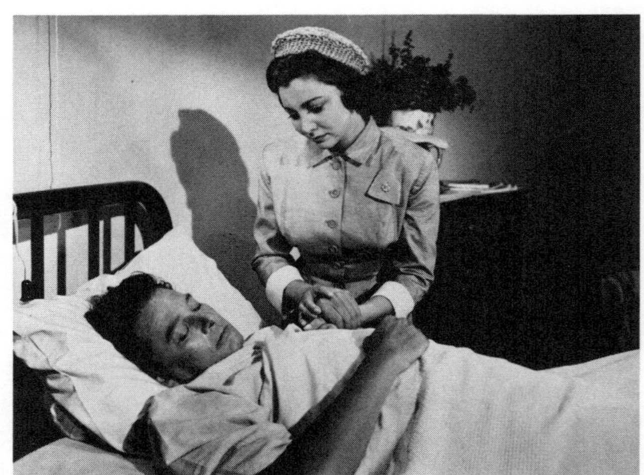

Hollywood Thrill Makers. Stuntman Bill Henry got sympathy from Theila Darin after almost breaking his neck. (Lippert, 1954)

Slim Carter. Jock Mahoney, Julie Adams, and Ben Johnson were in this story of a cowboy star heel who reforms. (U-I, 1957)

though he is terrified) rather than let down the visiting hero-worshipper.

The Fuzzy Pink Nightgown (1957) had Jane Russell playing a movie star who is kidnapped by Ralph Meeker and Keenan Wynn. In no time at all, Miss Russell, whose compassion passeth all logic, figures out why Meeker should do such an awful thing, and she even ends up reforming him.

Four Girls in Town (also 1957) was simply about four young aspiring actresses in Hollywood to test for a movie role: Julie Adams, Elsa Martinelli, Gia Scala, and Marianne Cook. Each had her romantic entanglements and her special reason for wanting to make it in the movies. George Nader played an assistant director (for whom Miss Adams falls) and virtually everyone in the film was nice. In fact, the movie tried so hard to suggest that everyone in Hollywood is decent, civilized, honor-

able, and dedicated to work that the movie capital came out seeming more like Carvel, where Judge Hardy's family lived.

And then there was *Kathy O'* (1958), with Patty McCormack as a monster of a movie moppet, making life miserable for publicist Dan Duryea, until we all find out the poor child really is not so bad, after all — just misunderstood.

Much bigger, though not necessarily better, was *Pepe* (1960), a star-laden exercise in gaudiness intended to capitalize on the earlier public acceptance of Cantinflas in *Around the World in 80 Days.* The Mexican comedy actor was cast as a ranch hand who is heartbroken when his favorite stallion is bought by visiting film director Dan Dailey. So Pepe simply tags along and soon gets involved in an inane plot about producers, directors, backers, starlets, gambling, etc.

Along the way, he has brief and usually pointless encounters with no less than twenty-eight "guest stars," including Bing Crosby, Jack Lemmon,

The Fuzzy Pink Nightgown. Film star Jane Russell takes a bite out of her abductor, Ralph Meeker. The script was fuzzier than the nightgown. (United Artists, 1957)

Four Girls in Town. George Nader, arms folded, and Julie Adams, second from right, were the leads in this quadrupled Cinderella story. (U-I, 1957)

Kathy O'. Little Patty McCormack was a misunderstood movie moppet, but Dan Duryea and Mary Fickett helped straighten her out. (U-I, 1958)

Jimmy Durante, Maurice Chevalier, Frank Sinatra, Greer Garson and Zsa Zsa Gabor. But not all of Columbia's guest stars could make Pepe what it was supposed to be — a sequel to the flashy but infinitely more entertaining *Around the World in 80 Days.*

An offbeat item issued in 1961 was *Paradise Alley,* in which Hugo Haas as a has-been film director moved into an East Los Angeles ghetto and pretended to make a movie using neighborhood people. What makes it worthy of mention is that Haas, who also directed, assembled an interesting collection of movie old-timers to appear in the movie, including Chester Conklin, Corinne Griffith, Billy Gilbert, and Margaret Hamilton.

Pat Boone, who had been confined to white shoes and squeaky-clean roles, branched out a bit in *The Yellow Canary* (1963), playing a self-centered star who turned human — with a vengence — when his child was kidnapped.

In 1969, *The Comic* gave us a sometimes funny, sometimes sentimental view of a silent movie star (Dick Van Dyke) and the highs and lows of his life. Told in flashback — with Van Dyke in his own coffin narrating, as it were, from the great beyond

Pepe. Edward G. Robinson and Dan Dailey were only two
of the many guest stars in this limp Cantinflas vehicle.
(Columbia, 1960)

The Yellow Canary. Jack Klugman was the detective investigating the kidnapping of movie star Pat Boone's son. (20th Century-Fox, 1963)

The Comic. Aging comic Dick Van Dyke appears on the Steve Allen show to reminisce about his career in this affecting comedy-drama about a silent screen star who never knew when he was well off. (Columbia, 1969)

— it showed the comic as a complex, self-centered, rather stupid fellow, talented in his work, but a klutz in his personal relationships. Michele Lee was his long-suffering wife and later ex-wife; Mickey Rooney was excellent as his sidekick and pal. Parts of the film were devoted to carefully reconstructed silent comedy bits with these three performers.

But perhaps nothing in Carl Reiner's script said more about the character played by Van Dyke than one scene in which he boisterously invades his estranged wife's home determined to take away the young son for whom he claims to feel such strong love — and then abducts the wrong child. Touching, too, is a scene with Van Dyke as an old, washed-up has-been, visited at a senior citizens' home by his grown-up son, who turns out to be rather less manly than any father would hope for.

Mostly, the film treated this foolish comedian with compassion, and even if it was uneven and sometimes reached too far for its effects, it was a curiously affecting study of a man never quite big enough for his own boots.

Although it was by no means the best movie about a Hollywood personality with a heart, in a way *The Comic* summed up what the movies have been trying to tell us, from time to time, about its own people — that inside even the most offensive monster there dwells an imperfect human being.

And in *The Comic*, whatever its flaws, this is shown through the classic portrait of a clown whose gaudy makeup hides an insecure heart.

5 Hollywood Exposes Hollywood

Like any other community in the United States, Hollywood has always enjoyed a good scandal. Also like any other community, the closer to home the scandal is, the better.

Back in the days when Louella Parsons and Hedda Hopper used to titillate their millions of readers by chronicling the madcap activities of the stars, or "scoop" each other with the very first whisper of the latest liaison, affair, marriage, divorce, or brawl involving show business personalities, those show business personalities were themselves among the gossip columnists' most constant readers.

Even now, when Joyce Haber* and Rona Barrett have succeeded Lolly and Hedda, the movie "colony" is as aware as the rest of the readers of what the latest gossip is. Now, as then, some high-priced publicity agents make a good living by planting items in the columns, Hollywood having always existed on the theory that what a columnist says about you is not as important as just being mentioned.

There is a classic, though possibly apochryphal, story about the press agent of an actor calling up a columnist breathlessly reporting that his client had just been thrown from a horse and broken his leg. To which the jaded columnist reportedly replied:

*In 1975, the Los Angeles Times quietly dropped Haber's column.

"Sorry, Harry, I already mentioned him this week."

In any case, gossip and scandal have always been as much a part of Hollywood — in the minds of people out in the provinces as well as those in Hollywood — as lights, camera, action. It would seem to follow, then, that if an audience existed for movies about Hollywood, that audience could be even more surely enticed by a movie about Hollywood involving some sort of scandal.

This is not to say that every movie dealing with any sort of Hollywood scandal was guaranteed success. As with every other kind of film, there were successes and failures, films of quality and those that were unadulterated garbage, and quite a few that fell somewhere in between.

As to how many of these films bore any relationship to reality is another matter. To begin with, Hollywood was never the capital of film realism. Its history has been one of story-telling, glamorizing, giving America "escapist" entertainment, creating a world of Cinderellas in Cinderella stories, providing a magic carpet for America's moviegoers (and millions elsewhere) to ride away from their humdrum daily lives. What movie fans wanted in those days (and, in a way, in these days, too) was adventure, romance, excitement, scandal, mystery, action — anything, apparently, but reality.

Toward the goal of satisfying and increasing the moviegoing public, filmmakers were faced with the challenge of finding something "new" to present in story form — new and yet not untried.

If gossip, scandal, and crime sold newspapers, there was no reason they couldn't sell movies. And if the scandal could be made to seem "real" by involving actors playing actors in stories centered in Hollywood, so much the better, because it was already known that the public was that much more interested in gossip about celebrities than about nonentities.

For example, in 1923 Paramount released a film entitled *The World's Applause*, which bore more than a passing resemblance to a widely publicized authentic Hollywood scandal of the time — the murder of William Desmond Taylor, the film director whose lady friends had included Mary Miles Minter and Mabel Normand, both big Hollywood names then. In *The World's Applause*, Bebe Daniels played a star in love with Lewis Stone, who had a brief relationship (before meeting Stone) with Adolphe Menjou. Then Menjou's wife killed Menjou and Bebe was blamed. But in time she was cleared and she and Stone were reunited.

Even before that, the combination of scandalous crime and Hollywood glamor was used in *The Cinema Murder*, a 1920 Marion Davies film based on an E. Phillips Oppenheim book. Marion played a young actress who caught the fancy of an older man (Anders Randolph) but was really in love with a young actor (Nigel Barrie). She witnesses what looks like a murder and has reason to suspect young Barrie of committing it. But in the end, it turns out there never was a murder — just a terrible misunderstanding which, when explained, left Barrie pure of heart and thus acceptable to Marion.

If nothing else, *The Cinema Murder* proved that the subject of glamorous Hollywood people being involved in such unsavory activities was of interest to the public. And so, filmmakers periodically returned to that form of "expose" in movies.

The Studio Murder Mystery (1929) had an impressive cast that included Neil Hamilton, Warner Oland, Fredric March, Florence Eldridge, Eugene Pallette, and Chester Conklin. Although it dealt with the murder of a Hollywood actor, the film had a light touch, playing up the comic aspects of the mystery rather more than had been done in some earlier Hollywood murder yarns. March played a philandering actor, Oland was a

The World's Applause. Bebe Daniels and Adolphe Menjou were the stars of this early drama of love and murder. (Paramount, 1923)

The Cinema Murder. Anders Randolph and Marion Davies. Despite the menacing pose and the title, there was no murder. (Paramount, 1920)

The Studio Murder Mystery. Eugene Pallette was the stodgy detective, Neil Hamilton the brassy young man who solves the crime. (Paramount, 1929)

foreign-born director whose wife had been involved with the murder victim, Hamilton was the breezy type who was always one jump ahead of the police in trying to solve the crime.

Rather more somber was *The Lost Squadron* (1932) in which Erich von Stroheim, already famous as "the man you love to hate," played an imperious film director at work on a movie about flyers in the First World War. Three former flyers — played by Richard Dix, Joel McCrea, and Robert Armstrong — have jobs doing stunt flying in von Stroheim's film. Dix's former sweetheart (Mary Astor) is now married to von Stroheim, and the director, crazy with jealousy, plots to get rid of Dix in a convenient air accident. But it is Armstrong who is killed, McCrea who finds the incriminating evidence to fix the blame on von Stroheim, and Dix who survives the whole ugly mess.

Bela Lugosi's huge success as Count Dracula in 1931 forced him into a series of follow-up roles, all of them ghoulish. But in 1933 he escaped, temporarily, from the type-casting trap in a movie called *The Death Kiss.* This one went *The Studio Murder Mystery* one better in that it involved a murder on a studio set while they were making a movie about murder. Lugosi was understandably the most prominent suspect, and he must have been enormously pleased to have a role in which he turned out to be guiltless. Also in the cast were Adrienne Ames as a leading lady, and David Manners as the bright young screenwriter who solves the mystery.

(To further indicate the extent of Lugosi's scary

The Lost Squadron. **Mary Astor was married to Erich von Stroheim, but her heart belonged to another and Erich didn't like that. (RKO, 1932)**

The Death Kiss. Edward Van Sloan, Adrienne Ames, and Bela Lugosi were in this tale of murder on a movie set. (World Wide Pictures, 1933)

The Preview Murder Mystery. Rod LaRoque, Gail Patrick, George Barbier, and Ian Keith, all Hollywood types in yet another murder yarn. (Paramount, 1936)

image over the course of his career, I had the opportunity to interview him once, in the 1950's, and was most uneasy about the assignment. Lugosi had opened in Toronto in a stage play that I had reviewed — and not very favorably. The day after my review appeared in print, I got a phone call from Mr. Lugosi — that voice was frighteningly familiar — inviting me to join him for a drink later that day. We met at the lounge of his hotel and I half expected him to go for my jugular vein. He proved to be a charming man and we spent a pleasant hour or so together over drinks. Curiously, he neither mentioned the unfavorable review nor explained why he had invited me for a drink.)

The movie-within-a-movie technique was used again in *The Preview Murder Mystery* (1936), with Reginald Denny, Gail Patrick, Ian Keith, and Rod LaRoque heading the cast. LaRoque and Patrick were movie stars, Keith was the director, and only one of the murders in the movie occurred at a premiere. That was the shooting of LaRoque. Later, Keith was hanged, a night watchman was stabbed, and even Gail Patrick was almost bumped off before the crazed killer was apprehended.

By the 1940s, the B pictures had pretty well taken over the Hollywood crime exposé and, as might be expected, more than one "series" decided on a stop at the movie capital. One was *Boston Blackie* and another was *The Falcon*.

Chester Morris, who played Boston Blackie in a number of films in that series, was up to his usual unofficial sleuthing in *Boston Blackie Goes Hollywood* (1942). Along with his assistant (George E. Stone) he was called in to solve the disappearance of some valuable jewelry that Lloyd Corrigan had loaned to a starlet.

And in *The Falcon in Hollywood* (1944), Tom Conway, as the Falcon, was required to solve the murder of an actor. Also in the movie were Veda Ann Borg as a taxi driver and John Abbott as a Shakespeare-spouting producer.

George Brent and Joan Blondell played newspaper reporters working in Hollywood in *The Corpse Came C.O.D.* (1947). Behaving like typical movie reporters, they insisted on meddling into police business whan a couple of murders occur in a movie studio. But, as usual, it develops that the police could not have solved the case on their own, anyhow.

Slightly more inventive, at least in its approach to reflecting the Hollywood atmosphere, was *Heartaches* (1947), in which a crooner who could not really sing (Ken Farrell) receives letters threatening to expose his secret. Sheila Ryan appeared as the studio publicist, Edward Norris was the snoopy reporter who helped solve the ensuing murder, and Chill Wills* was the ghost singer for Farrell.

In 1951 came *Hollywood Story,* which was loosely based on the old William Desmond Taylor murder. Starring in it was Richard Conte as a film

*Wills later provided the voice for Francis, the Talking Mule.

Boston Blackie Goes Hollywood. **Chester Morris and George E. Stone, the two at right, had to solve a Hollywood crime when the police couldn't. (Columbia, 1942)**

producer bent on making a movie about the unsolved murder of a fictional director named Franklin Ferrara. To help add local color, the cast included such old-timers as Francis X. Bushman, Betty Blythe, William Farnum, and Helen Gibson — all playing themselves. In addition, Conte's "research" included screening Lon Chaney's *Phantom of the Opera.*

But the story was still B-Picture quality, with producer Conte getting sidetracked into solving the twenty-two-year-old murder instead of concentrating on his movie plans. Julia Adams was seen as the daughter of a silent screen star whose career had been ruined by the old scandal surrounding the murder. Fred Clark was Conte's backer, behaving suspiciously enough to insure that he was not the murderer. And Henry Hull played a has-been

The Falcon in Hollywood. **Tom Conway, center, was the noted sleuth, and Veda Ann Borg his favorite cab driver. (RKO, 1944)**

The Corpse Came C.O.D. Detective Fred Sears needs Hollywood reporters George Brent and Joan Blondell to find the killer. (Columbia, 1947)

Heartaches. Edward Norris, center, was a reporter going after the blackmailer of a star. At right is Sheila Ryan. (PRC, 1947)

Hollywood Story. **Richard Conte, looking up, started out as a producer, ended packing a rod. (U-I, 1951)**

screenwriter hired by Conte to do the script of the Ferrara story.

Representing the forces of law and order was Richard Egan as a detective with a flair for philosophical observations like: "An unsolved murder case is never closed."

The same year, Mickey Rooney, too far past puberty to masquerade any longer as Andy Hardy, played a musician in *The Strip* (1951), referring to Hollywood's famed Sunset Strip, then the area of swinging night spots. Rooney was in love with Sally Forrest, who had movie ambitions that were encouraged by a no-goodnik (James Craig) who kept promising to get her a screen test. It took most of the picture and a good bit of violence before Sally came to her senses and realized Mickey was worth more than any silly old movie career.

Night Without Sleep (1952) had Gary Merrill as a composer who wakes up with a humdinger of a hangover and the nagging feeling that he killed someone the night before. But was it his shrewish wife (June Vincent), his tempestuous mistress (Hildegarde Neff), or the beautiful movie star (Linda Darnell) with whom he had once been romantically involved? The mystery is eventually cleared up, but the only thing that might be said in defense of this dreary movie was that at least it did not reach out into left field for a trick ending. Merrill had indeed dispatched one of the ladies — his wife.

Hugo Haas, the Czech-born actor who later became a writer-director as well, dealt with Hollywood-based exposé in *The Other Woman* (1955). Haas played a producer-director who got his break by marrying the boss's daughter. Cleo Moore portrayed an extra girl out for revenge because Haas had rejected her plea for work. Cleo is murdered after blackmailing Haas, so, of course, he is the prime suspect when she is killed.

Not all Hollywood exposé movies concerned themselves with murder. Attractive though murder mysteries may be to both filmmakers and writers

The Strip. Mickey Rooney and William Demarest were in this melodrama of Hollywood greed. (MGM, 1951)

of fiction, there are other kinds of juicy scandal inextricably associated with Hollywood; so it is to be expected that some movies would take note of these.

An example was _Hollywood Boulevard_ (1936), in which John Halliday played a passé matinee idol who tries to pretend he is still a celebrity in demand. In desperation, he allows himself to be persuaded by a publishing huckster to write his memoirs. The printed revelations cause considerable embarrassment to Halliday's former wife, his daughter, and even the wife of the unscrupulous publisher, herself, it seems, a conquest of Halliday's in his heyday. Marsha Hunt played Halliday's daughter, and Robert Cummings was around to console her. The publisher and his wife were portrayed by C. Henry Gordon and Freida Inescourt.

Night Without Sleep. Linda Darnell was a film star from Gary Merrill's past in this potboiler. (20th Century-Fox, 1952)

The Other Woman. Cleo Moore had the title role, Hugo Haas was the ruthless producer-director. (20th Century-Fox, 1955)

Kay Francis, who had been a reasonably big star in the 1930s, made her last film in 1946. Entitled *Wife Wanted,* it cast her as an aging movie star (a euphemism within a euphemism) who invests the last of her money in a real estate firm, only to discover that the company is a front for a shady lonely hearts club. Paul Cavanaugh played her crooked business partner, who later turned murderer, and Robert Shayne was the nice reporter who saved both Kay and her money.

In the 1950s, scandal magazines were all the rage, and Hollywood gossip was a staple without which such rags would have had a much smaller audience than they did. The subject of such magazines and their tactics provided the basis for *Slander* (1957), with Van Johnson as a children's entertainer on television who is blackmailed by

Hollywood Boulevard. Marsha Hunt and Robert Cummings were the romantic leads of this exposé-type story. (Paramount, 1936)

112

Wife Wanted. Kay Francis was a fading star who backed into all kinds of trouble in this inferior melodrama. (Monogram, 1946)

Slander. Ann Blyth stuck with Van Johnson through thick and thin in this expose´ of scandal magazines. (MGM, 1957)

sneering smear magazine publisher Steve Cochran, as a means of getting some dirt on a childhood friend of Johnson's who is now a famous actress. Ann Blyth played Johnson's loyal wife in this simplistic melodrama, and both she and Johnson were far better than the script.

The scandal magazine racket got another working over in *Secret File Hollywood* (1962), with Robert Clarke as a private eye who goes to work for such a publication when he loses his license. There, he learns about such sordid goings-on as photographer Francine York's assignment to get compromising pictures of a movie director and an actress for blackmail purposes. Clarke ends up working as an undercover police agent to dig up the evidence that will put the magazine out of business.

As it has done in other fields, Hollywood thus used its own medium of communication to discredit the scandal magazines that had done their best to smear a number of Hollywood personalities. Such publications still exist, naturally, but their hold on show business celebrities is less strong now than it was twenty years ago, and it is possible some of the movies mentioned above had something to do with informing the public that not every word appearing in print is necessarily gospel. Or, possibly, today's public is less easily shocked by revelations concerning celebrities and less inclined to boycott the films of idols who are revealed to have clay feet.

It is not the intention of this survey, however, to suggest that the vast propaganda machinery available to Hollywood has invariably been used for humane purposes. Indeed, moviemakers have been known to bend a few facts — or stories — in order to make the Hollywood image retain both its glamor and its respectability.

On more than one occasion, Broadway plays that needled or otherwise ridiculed Hollywood were bought up and filmed, but with basic and self-serving alterations. A couple of examples will illustrate the point.

Back in 1936, "Stage Door," a play by Edna Ferber and George S. Kaufman, was one of the big hits of the season. Set in a theatrical boarding house in New York, it told of a group of young actresses trying to crash Broadway. Much of the Kaufman wit was aimed at what he regarded as the shallowness of Hollywood. In fact, one of the ambitious actresses in the play "sells out" by going to Hollywood — Kaufman and Ferber made it sound like the equivalent of signing up with a bordello — and even the bright, honest playwright is lured to the West Coast fleshpots. Both return to New York totally corrupted by the Hollywood lifestyle and glitter. Only our heroine remains loyal to The Theater, even though it means working as a salesgirl and hounding agents' offices. But justice triumphs: the actress who became a movie star is back to do a Broadway play, but she is so bad in rehearsal that she is dumped, and guess who replaces her and becomes a real star of the legitimate theatah?

When the film version of *Stage Door* was released the following year, it still dealt with the

113

Secret File Hollywood. **Robert Clarke, left, went under-
ground to break up a ring of Hollywood extortionists.
(Crown-International, 1962)**

trials and tribulations of budding actresses. But the
whole Hollywood business was eliminated; the
triumphs, defeats, and heartbreak all had to do
with Broadway, and the only villain was a big
Broadway producer too busy and too self-impor-
tant to recognize all the budding talent around
him. The film, with Katharine Hepburn, Ginger
Rogers, Adolphe Menjou, and Gail Patrick in the
leading roles, was every bit as big a hit as the play
had been — despite the fact that the Hollywood
angle had been totally exorcised.

The other example of Hollywood's defensive
plot-switching occurred twenty years later, in
1957. First, there was the Broadway play, in this
case *Will Success Spoil Rock Hunter?*, by George
Axelrod. It was about a meek reporter (Orson
Bean) assigned to interview a Hollywood sexpot
(Jayne Mansfield). He meets an agent who, for
successive ten percent hunks of the reporter's soul,
arranges for the blonde star to fall in love with the

Stage Door. **Katharine Hepburn, Adolphe Menjou, and
Ginger Rogers were the leads in this Hollywood switch of
an anti-Hollywood play. (RKO, 1937)**

Will Success Spoil Rock Hunter? Tony Randall, Jayne Mansfield, and Joan Blondell helped prove that it did. (20th Century-Fox, 1957)

reporter, writes a screenplay for him, and even sets him up to win an Oscar. In the nick of time, Rock Hunter manages to free himself from both the love Goddess and Hollywood. The play was successful enough to be sold to the movies, but little more than the title was left unaltered.

The movie version had Jayne Mansfield again, and Tony Randall played the title role. But now Rock Hunter was an advertising man trying to con the movie queen into endorsing a lipstick on behalf of his client. He succeeds in this, is made famous with the help of Jayne and ends up as president of the advertising company. In short, the whole plot was switched around to satirize the advertising game and television, with nary a mention of movies. But apart from helping to launch Randall's and Miss Mansfield's movie careers, the film was not especially noteworthy.

(There are, of course, numerous other examples of Hollywood "switches" — from changing the Japanese film classic, Rashomon, into a routine Western entitled *The Outrage,* to changing the sex of Rudyard Kipling's Wee Willie Winkie to accommodate Shirley Temple. But we're dealing here with movies about Hollywood and its citizens.)

Happily, some of Hollywood's best films exposing Hollywood needed no such switches or gimmicks, nor did they rely on the hokey plots that characterized many of the films referred to up to now in this category.

Since many of these better movies were made in the 1950s, one is tempted to conclude that Hollywood was by then showing signs of maturity in its treatment of its most famous industry and the people who inhabited it. But then again there have been some duds in the same decade — and since — so perhaps it is too early to draw any conclusions.

One of the most unusual and honest of these films was *In a Lonely Place* (1950), with

115

Humphrey Bogart and Gloria Grahame in the leading roles. Ironically, despite the Bogart cult that has emerged since that star's death, this film is generally excluded from the list of favorite Bogie movies, yet it provided him with one of his strongest roles, which he played admirably.

Bogart was a screenwriter with a violent streak in his nature that periodically jeopardized his career. Assigned to do the screenplay of a book he has not yet read, he invites a hatcheck girl (Martha Stewart) to tell him the story of the book when he learns she has read it. When the girl is later found murdered, Bogart is a prime suspect until neighbor Gloria Grahame tells the police that she witnessed Bogart putting the girl into a cab after she had been in Bogart's apartment. Before long, Gloria has virtually moved in with Bogart, helping him with his script, cooking his meals, and otherwise comforting him. But recurrent bursts of violence plague Bogart and in time Gloria begins to have doubts about him — even as to whether or not he killed the hatcheck girl. By the time the murder is solved (Bogart was innocent of it) his relationship with Gloria is so damaged that they go their separate ways, she to wonder about the nature of this brooding man, he to continue his stormy, unhappy life.

It was a moody film, one in which the character so ably played by Bogart remains something of an enigma. But it conveyed such a sense of honesty in dealing with its imperfectly human characters that it won high critical praise, if not box-office popularity. And the supporting cast, including Frank Lovejoy, Jeff Donnell, and Robert Warwick, was uniformly good.

It could not have been merely the unhappy ending that doomed *In a Lonely Place* to failure, for the same year brought another Hollywood movie which, even with an unhappy ending, proved enormously successful and enduringly popular.

This was the Billy Wilder film in which Gloria Swanson made her big 1950 comeback, *Sunset Boulevard.* It was, in the fullest sense, an exposé of a particular aspect of Hollywood life: the pathetic story of a silent screen star living in a dream world, convinced she will one day make her big comeback. Who could doubt that there dwelt in Hollywood or Beverly Hills at least one such dreamer?

Swanson played Norma Desmond (even the name sounded like that of a silent screen star), living in a rundown mansion with Erich von Stroheim, once her director and husband, now merely her butler and worshipper. Into this strange menage stumbles William Holden, a screenwriter barely one jump ahead of the bill collectors. Against his better judgment but motivated by his own greed, he agrees to stay on, earning a salary, to work on a script with which the divine Desmond hopes to recrack the film world.

All three principals were splendid from start to finish, but so were Wilder's direction and the sparkling script provided by Wilder, Charles Brackett, and D.M. Marshman, Jr.

"You were big," says Holden when he first realizes he is in the presence of the great Norma Desmond.

"I *am* big," she corrects him. "It's the pictures that got small."

And von Stroheim, still adoring her even while recognizing, perhaps even sharing, her madness, describes her to Holden this way: "She was the greatest of them all. One week she got 17,000 fan letters. A maharaja came all the way from India for one of her silk stockings. Later he strangled himself with it."

To further achieve a convincing ambience, Wilder studded his cast with a brace of old-timers playing themselves: Hedda Hopper, Anna Q. Nillson, Buster Keaton, H.B. Warner, and the ubiquitous Cecil B. DeMille.

Sunset Boulevard crackled with Wilder's sense of irony, evoking more sympathy for the faded glamor queen, removed though she was from reality, than for the ambitious young writer who took her money while ridiculing her dream. Perhaps Holden's death was not really an "unhappy" ending after all, only a just one.

Two years later, in 1953, Bette Davis came up with a strong performance in a movie called *The Star.* The character she played was, in a way, a glimpse of what Norma Desmond might have been through before succumbing to her particular dementia.

Davis played Margaret Elliott, a onetime Oscar winner now on the way down, well past her prime but not yet aware of this, or at least unable to face it. Broke, denied work, saddled with parasitic relatives, and weighed down by her own vision of her greatness, she is incapable of coping with the new reality — that the days of glamor and adulation are over, that she is no longer The Star.

In a Lonely Place. Humphrey Bogart, Gloria Grahame, and Art Smith in a scene from one of the more underrated Bogie films. (Columbia, 1950)

This acute study of a woman caught up in the myth of her own immortality offered Davis her meatiest role since *All About Eve.* If the film had a major failing, it was the dragging in of a strong and sympathetic man (Sterling Hayden) primarily for the purpose of setting up the story's rather unconvincing happy ending.

But along the way, we got a clear look at a woman so wrapped up in her own legend that she cannot conceive of the possibility of any other way of life; on the one hand all too aware that her merry-go-round ride is ended, yet on the other still clutching desperately at one more chance to prove she can still be glamorous and desirable to an audience that has already lost interest in her.

An even more searing exposé of Hollywood was the Clifford Odets film, based on his own play, *The Big Knife* (1955). Jack Palance was the star in this movieland drama, fighting to break the studio's iron grip on his career. To add to his troubles, his wife (Ida Lupino) is about to leave him, fed up with his casual infidelities.

With a heavy hand, Odets mixed in an assortment of villains chilling enough to fan the flame in any Hollywood hater's heart. Chief among them was Rod Steiger as the despotic studio head, a megalomaniac of grand proportions, suitably portrayed with Steigeresque flamboyance.

Then there was Wendell Corey as Steiger's trouble shooter, a henchman who does not flinch at murder to rid his boss of a loud-mouthed party girl (Shelley Winters) who has rocked the boat. And there was also Ilka Chase as a gossip columnist all too eager to confirm in print the rumors of a split between Palance and his wife.

Sunset Boulevard. Old smoothie Cecil B. DeMille knew just how to handle ex-movie queen Gloria Swanson in this superior movieland drama. (Paramount, 1950)

The Star. Bette Davis was perfect as the movie star on her way down. With her above is Sterling Hayden. (20th Century-Fox, 1953)

The Big Knife. Confrontation between studio hatchet man Wendell Corey and moody star Jack Palance. (United Artists, 1955)

Apart from overemphasizing the evil in these villains, the movie's biggest problem was its failure to make very clear what it was that Palance was so determined to escape, so unable to live with that he ends up a suicide.

Budd Schulberg, another writer who, like Odets, had ample opportunity to observe Hollywood up close, came through with a fascinating study of a star with virtually no scruples in *A Face in the Crowd* (1957). The star (Andy Griffith) gained his fame via television rather than films, but the public adoration of this fraudulently homespun character is not much different from that showered on movie stars.

Griffith starts out as a hillbilly entertainer, discovered by Patricia Neal, who rises to the very heights of show business success, shrewdly showing the public his best side, his lack of pretention, his down-home humanity. But we, the audience, see also his treachery, his thirst for power, his willingness to use anyone in his climb to stardom.

Well written, tautly directed (by Elia Kazan) and brilliantly acted by Griffith, *A Face in the Crowd* offered an intimate look at a monster so successful that he dominates the media magicians who helped create him; so amoral that he can and does turn the public's gullibility to his own advantage. When Patricia Neal, convinced that he must be destroyed, throws the switch that suddenly exposes the man's true nature to his astonished public, one could hardly find any reason for pitying him.

A far more sympathetic view of stardom was Paddy Chayefsky's original screenplay, *The Goddess,* made in 1958, with Kim Stanley in the title role of a lonely woman whose pathetic search for love leads her to Hollywood stardom but not at all to happiness.

Chayefsky's heroine is a victim not so much of Hollywood as of a cold and loveless childhood whose insecurity prompts her to daydream of a glamorous career as a film star. But the realization of that dream fails to stem the girl's emotional

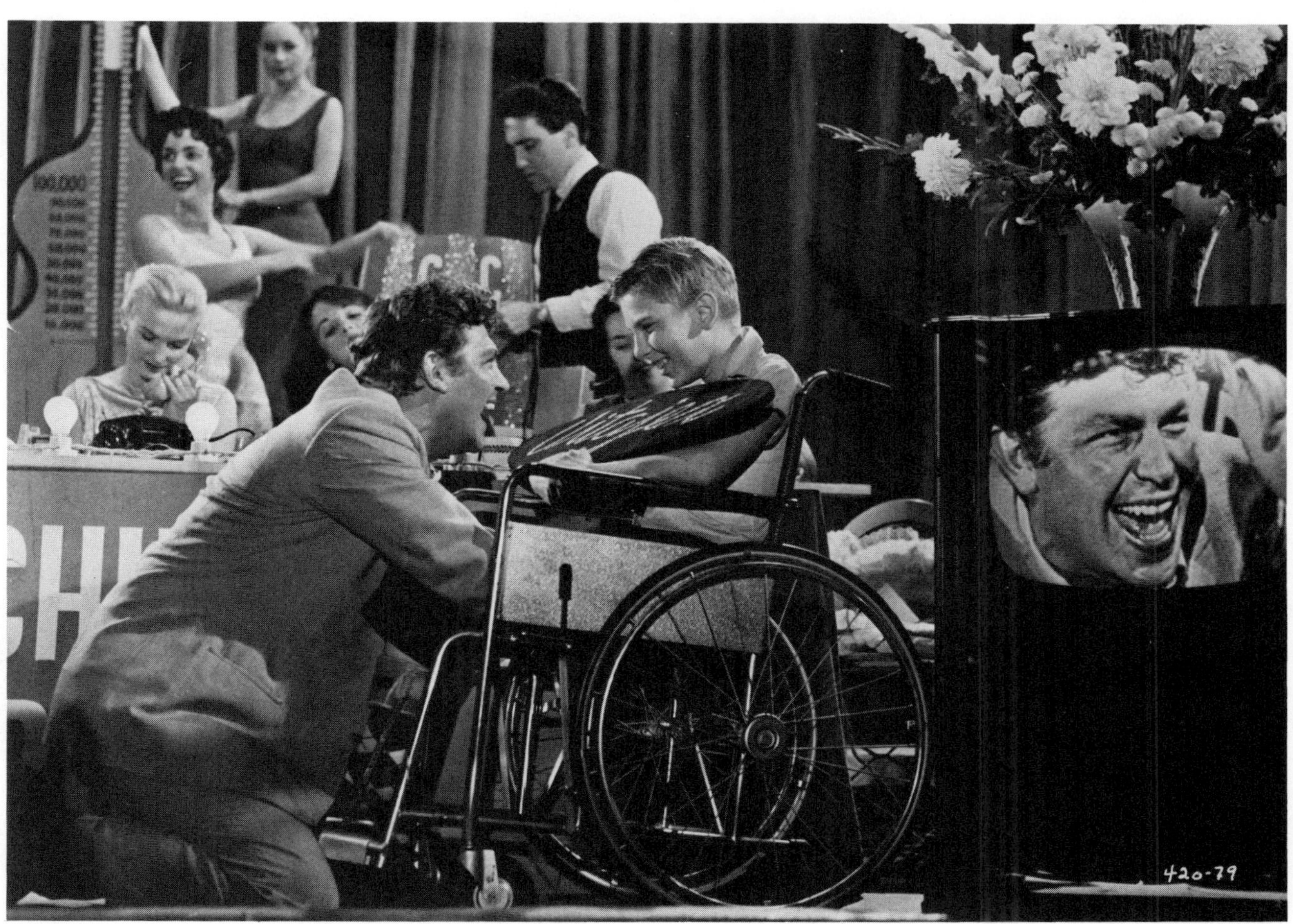

A Face in the Crowd. **Television idol Andy Griffith turns on the charm for a crippled boy. (Warner Brothers, 1957)**

deterioration. Nor does a futile marriage to a hapless exfighter (Lloyd Bridges) help any.

What *The Goddess* reveals is the emptiness of a life that some might consider fulfilling. There were those who found a parallel between the Kim Stanley role and the stormy career of Marilyn Monroe, who had, by then, been married to and divorced from exballplayer Joe DiMaggio, and whose erratic behavior was already suggesting considerable emotional instability. In any case, it was a sad and depressing film, intelligently written and ably acted by Miss Stanley.

These last half-dozen films, ranging from *In a Lonely Place* to *The Goddess*, would tend to indicate that Hollywood in the 1950s had gained some insight as to its own problems, shortcomings, and traps. More important, it was not the least bit shy about exposing its seamier side to public view.

But not all of this periodic introspection yielded such enlightening results. There were also shoddy and spurious films dealing with Hollywood, films designed more to exploit to the fullest the public's appetite for exposé, or to sentimentalize Hollywood life. These included *Slander* and *Secret File Hollywood,* already mentioned.

One that defies categorization was *The Man Who Understood Women* (1959), a Nunnally Johnson effort with Henry Fonda and Leslie Caron. Although filmed on the French Riviera, it concerned Hollywood people. Fonda was a filmmaker who had molded Caron into a big star, then married her. They were in Nice to make a new picture, despite her reluctance to work any further. The husband's blindness to his wife's yearning for

The Goddess. **Kim Stanley glowed in this drama of loneliness in filmland. Her companion above is Lloyd Bridges. (Columbia, 1958)**

domesticity drove her into an affair with a soldier (Cesare Danova). Neither critics nor public found the film satisfying, despite some brisk dialogue by Johnson.

The same year brought us *Beloved Infidel*, with Deborah Kerr as Hollywood gossip columnist Sheila Graham and Gregory Peck as F. Scott Fitzgerald. Miss Graham had earlier committed her memoirs to paper in a book that was of more than passing interest since it dealt, in part, with her rambling love affair with the legendary idol of the lost generation.

Fitzgerald was well on the skids when he and Miss Graham found each other, and so the movie dwelt at some length on his drinking and brawling as well as the torment she suffered at seeing this once-revered writer, now her lover, disintegrate. But neither the script, which indulged in much name-dropping, nor the superficial performances of the stars did much to raise it above the level of soap opera. It reminded one of the old joke about the elderly Catholic woman who confessed to her priest the details of an illicit love affair she had had a half century ago, on the grounds that she still liked to think about it.

Another book of the time yielded a totally different sort of Hollywood exposé film. This was *Man on a String* (1960) from the book *Ten Years a Counterspy*, by Boris Morros. The Russian-born composer and later film producer had been a famous name in Hollywood for many years when he wrote his startling book, which revealed he had spent a decade as an undercover FBI agent posing as a Soviet spy.

His book was turned into a compelling suspense film, thanks partly to the authentic cloak-and-

The Man Who Understood Women. Henry Fonda played the title role in this amusing but confusing film. (20th Century-Fox, 1959)

Beloved Infidel. Deborah Kerr was Sheila Graham and Gregory Peck her beloved F. Scott Fitzgerald. (20th Century-Fox, 1959)

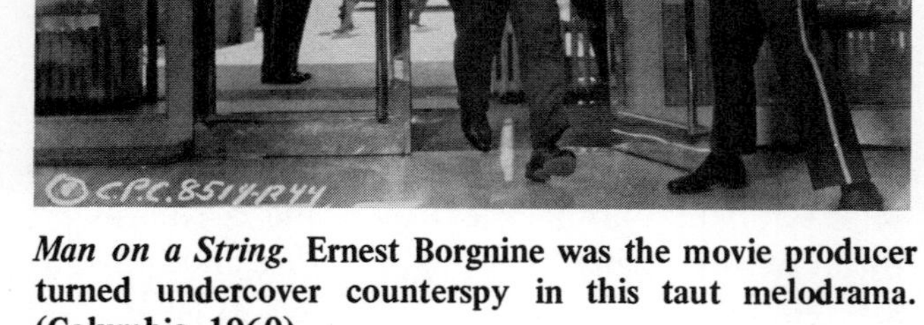

Man on a String. Ernest Borgnine was the movie producer turned undercover counterspy in this taut melodrama. (Columbia, 1960)

dagger adventures involved, and partly to the approach to the production adopted by Louis de Rochemont, a past master at documentary-type thrillers. Ernest Borgnine appeared as Morros and gave his usual dependable performance.

In 1962, *Sweet Bird of Youth,* from a Tennessee Williams play, gave us a graphic portrait of a couple of unsavory Hollywood types — an amoral Hollywood hustler who lives off a fading movie queen, and the grotesque lady who supports him. These two, played by Paul Newman and Geraldine Page, land in Newman's Southern hometown because Newman still hankers for the sweet young girl he left behind. From there on, the story had much more to do with the sordid relationships of all the main characters than it did with Hollywood.

But Miss Page's version of a degenerate Hollywood has-been was at least worth the watching, even if Mr. Williams's plot seemed unnecessarily murky.

More unsavory Hollywood people on location were dissected in *Two Weeks in Another Town* (1962), from an Irwin Shaw novel. The setting was Rome, and the characters included a washed-up film actor (Kirk Douglas), his predatory ex-wife (Cyd Charisse), a director of spear-and-sandals epics (Edward G. Robinson), a young actor too lazy to work (George Hamilton), and the director's possessive wife (Claire Trevor).

After Robinson has a heart attack, he appoints Douglas to finish directing the film, a reasonably unlikely assignment that Douglas carries out in his best Frank Gorshin style. Whatever the merits of

Shaw's novel may have been, most of them were muddled in this gaudy movie.

Closer to home, *The Female Animal* (1958) offered us Hedy Lamarr as a movie queen with a drinking problem who hires George Nader as the caretaker of her sumptuous beach house. Miss Lamarr's daughter (Jane Powell), who also has a fondness for the bottle, comes along and shows interest in Mama's caretaker. After a good deal of chatter — some of it convincingly Hollywoodesque — Lamarr steps aside to let her daughter have Nader. The other characterization of note was that by Jan Sterling, as an actress no longer in demand.

One of the freak hits of 1962 was *What Ever Happened to Baby Jane?*, a mock horror film with Bette Davis and Joan Crawford as two demented sisters living in a spooky house and doting on the days when both were child stars. Crawford is confined to a wheelchair, the result of an accident presumably caused by Davis. Later, it develops that Crawford engineered her own accident in a way to make it look as though Davis was responsible. Davis, meanwhile, has plans for a comeback and hires Victor Buono to write some musical arrangements for her. The film is peppered with gory violence, implausible plot twists, and two dazzlingly bravura performances by the stars. Though nobody could take it very seriously, a great many people went to see it for fun and thrills — and came away satisfied.

(Back in 1958, another mock horror film with a Hollywood setting came along, but failed to make much of an impression. This was *How to Make a*

122

Sweet Bird of Youth. Geraldine Page and Paul Newman, two Hollywood predators on a sordid spree. (MGM, 1962)

Monster, with Robert H. Harris as a studio makeup man who is fired by a new management and plots a grisly revenge involving a combination of makeup and hypnotic suggestion to force actors to commit the crimes he demands.)

In 1964 came one of Hollywood's most successful exposé films, *The Carpetbaggers,* based on the equally popular Harold Robbins book. It traced the career of an aviation tycoon turned film producer (vaguely suggesting Howard Hughes) and his encounters with a sexpot he turns into a star (Carroll Baker), a wife he leaves and then returns to (Elizabeth Ashley), a rugged old character of dubious background who is built into a big Western star (Alan Ladd), and assorted lesser Hollywood figures.

The central character was played by George Peppard with rather more stoicism than seemed

Two Weeks in Another Town. Kirk Douglas, Claire Trevor, and Edward G. Robinson were among the movie types on location in Italy. (MGM, 1962)

The Female Animal. George Nader and Hedy Lamarr think they've found love in Malibu, but it was only a flesh wound. (U-I, 1958)

What Ever Happened to Baby Jane? Joan Crawford and Bette Davis chewed up all the scenery in this Hollywood Gothic. (Warner Brothers, 1962)

How to Make a Monster. Robert Harris and Paul Brininger were the Hollywood equivalents of the mad scientist and his trusted Igor. (American-International, 1958)

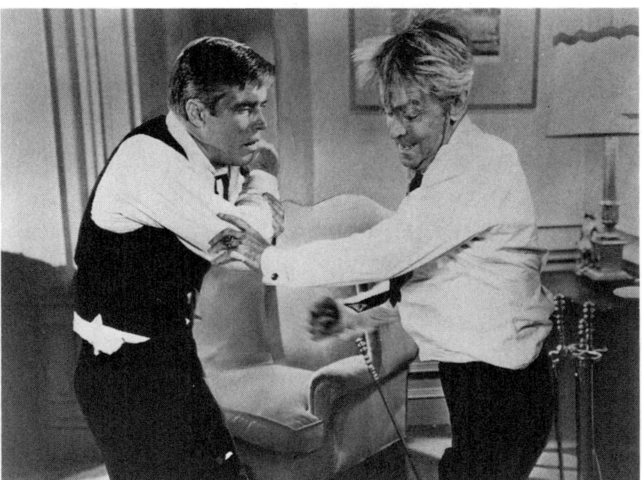

The Carpetbaggers. George Peppard and Alan Ladd slug it out in this scene from the steamy Harold Robbins yarn. (Paramount, 1964)

The Loved One. Even Liberace couldn't smile in this heavy-handed version of Evelyn Waugh's famous tale. (MGM, 1965)

called for, and the film abounded in near-sensational incidents designed to give the public exactly the kind of titillating detail of Hollywood life they were expecting.

Others in the large cast were Robert Cummings as an unctuous Hollywood agent, Martha Hyers as a starlet of nudies, Martin Balsam as a producer, and Lew Ayres as a lawyer.

The Carpetbaggers was a kind of Peyton Place West, but it was a big success largely because it lived up to the public's image of what life in Hollywood was supposed to be like — according to the gossip columnists and scandal magazines.

As for what death in Hollywood was supposed to be like, we were treated to that in *The Loved One* (1964), the ads for which boasted that it had something to offend everyone. Rarely has a movie lived up to its advertising as faithfully as this one did.

Based on an old Evelyn Waugh satire about the burial customs of the movie colony, this gross picture tried so hard to be outrageously funny that it succeeded in being outrageously dull. Screenwriters Terry Southern and Christopher Isherwood, and director Tony Richardson contrived to turn Waugh's rapier into a bludgeon.

Among the bizarre characters were Robert Morse, as a naive young British poet working in a Hollywood animal crematorium; Sir John Gielgud as Morse's uncle, a studio head who commits suicide; Rod Steiger, as a repulsive embalmer; Jonathan Winters in a dual role, one part unfunnier than the other; Liberace as a grinning coffin salesman; Robert Morley as a spokesman for the British colony in Hollywood; and Milton Berle and Margaret Leighton as a couple mourning the death of their pet.

They all pranced through their paces somewhat self-consciously, as if they were dimly aware that they were appearing in an over-stuffed turkey.

By the mid-1960s Hollywood exposés were becoming more sordid, less subtle, no doubt in accordance with the new awareness that audiences seemed to want more shocks per reel than ever before.

Back in 1937, we had *A Star is Born*, a romantic but generally satisfying "inside" story of the heartbreak of stardom. That film was remade, and better, in 1954, with Judy Garland and James Mason.

Now, in 1966, we got *Inside Daisy Clover*,

another rags-to-riches-to-misery Hollywood yarn, but with paper-thin characters from start to finish. Daisy Clover (played with minimum believability by Natalie Wood) is one of those golden-hearted urchins living with her eccentric mother (Ruth Gordon) in a shack near Venice Beach, in Los Angeles.

She sends an amateur recording of her singing voice to a studio nabob, and almost before you can say "a star is born" a limousine pulls up at the shack carrying Christopher Plummer, all set to sign up Natalie to a long term contract. A couple of production montages later, Natalie is an unhappy star, moping around the home of the studio head and his neurotic wife.

Next, she falls in love with and marries a dashing young actor (Robert Redford) who turns out to be a homosexual, and Natalie has what her particular muse has led her to believe we will accept as a breakdown. It was no more impressive than her singing on that amateur recording.

In a sense, the most masochistic exposé of Hollywood ever was *The Oscar* (1966), if only because it dared to cast a shadow across one of the movie industry's most sacred cows — the annual Academy Awards. That it did so cheaply, shoddily, with more cliches than one would find in a B Western of the 1930s, made it all the worse.

The film centered about the annual award ceremony and the frantic attempts of its hero-heel (Stephen Boyd) to make sure he wins an Oscar. Boyd is shown as a thoroughly despicable man, selfish, unprincipled, and vain. He is surrounded by such stock characters as the ruthless studio head (Joseph Cotten), the philosophical agent (Milton Berle), the smitten drama coach (Eleanor Parker), the sexy wife (Elke Sommer), and the loyal friend who is betrayed (Tony Bennett).

Even more depressing was the presence of such solid Hollywood citizens as Bob Hope, Merle Oberon, and Frank Sinatra, lending their presence to this hollow enterprise, appearing as themselves

Inside Daisy Clover. Natalie Wood was Daisy and Christopher Plummer the mogul who discovered her. (Warner Brothers, 1966)

The Oscar. Joseph Cotten's desk was probably as artificial as the story. With him above are Eleanor Parker and Milton Berle. (Embassy, 1966)

in the Academy Awards scene that climaxes the dreary film. Nor did the fact that the character played by Boyd fail to win his Oscar do much to mitigate the tastelessness of the whole venture.

For Hollywood, it was a little bit like a heartless mother charging admission for morbid crowds to view her six-fingered child.

The following year, yet another sordid exposé movie came along, this time from Jacqueline Susann's enormously popular book, *Valley of the Dolls.* Miss Susann concentrated on the rising use of pills ("dolls") among show business types, as the latest form of depravity gripping the entertainment world.

But her characters were plagued with other problems as well, ranging from massive egos to breast cancer. And most of them behaved like characters in a daytime serial — only with more freedom of expression than is usually allowed on soap operas.

Barbara Parkins was the sweet young thing from Massachusetts who lands in New York and promptly gets a job with a show biz lawyer, simultaneously capturing the eye of Paul Burke, an agent. She witnesses the crushing of Patty Duke's budding career at the hands of a jealous star (Susan Hayward). After an affair with Burke, Barbara is "discovered" by Charles Drake and made a cosmetic commercial girl on television.

Meanwhile, young Miss Duke has managed to survive the low blow from Hayward and becomes a film star. She marries Martin Milner, who sits around her pool aimlessly while Patty pops pills to keep going. When he walks out on her, Patty tells him: "Success is too big for you."

Agent Burke has also arranged for a screen career for singer Tony Scotti, who loves Sharon Tate. But Tony's sister (Lee Grant) tries to break up their romance, knowing that her brother has "a terminal illness." But the two kids get married anyhow, and later Sharon has to go to France and work in nudie films to help pay for Tony's hospital bills — until she finds she has breast cancer.

Valley of the Dolls. Paul Burke and Barbara Parkins face the press, including Jacqueline Susann, who wrote the original book. (20th Century-Fox, 1967)

That was the way it went for a couple of hours, and when it was all over, what we had learned was that pills, stardom, and cancer are bad for you.

Thus, Hollywood had advanced from rather naive exposés in the 1920s and 1930s, in which murders either were solved by amiable visiting sleuths or did not happen at all, to the films of the 1960s like *The Carpetbaggers, The Oscar,* and *Valley of the Dolls,* in which depravity, corruption, greed, and double-crossing were celebrated as the "inside" elements of Hollywood.

One might suppose that the filmmakers were becoming masochists, displaying their seediest aspects for the perverse pleasure such exhibitionism brought them. But commercial considerations could not be excluded.

Just as the makers of *The Cinema Murder,* in 1920, sensed that a murder story based in Hollywood was sure to attract audiences, so did the film makers of the 1960s believe that sordid, ugly revelations about Hollywood types would find box-office approval in these days of increased candor about everybody's hang-ups.

It might be argued that the makers of these later films did not serve Hollywood's image well. But perhaps, from the film industry's viewpoint, even destructive movies were better than no movies at all — so long as people would pay to see them.

6 Hollywood Salutes the Boys

When the Second World War came along, or more correctly, when the United States got into it, Hollywood turned itself into a vast propaganda machine, churning out action films that were part sentiment, part recruiting poster, part patriotism.

The anti-Axis or pro-Allies movies covered a lot of territory, from *Objective Burma* to *The Moon is Down*, from *Destination Tokyo* to *The Story of G.I. Joe*, from *Guadalcanal Diary* to *Casablanca*, from *Air Force* to *Desert Victory*, from *Wake Island* to *Bataan* to *The Purple Heart*.

Some of these were memorable dramas, capturing the essence of war, focussing on the very real sacrifices being made by millions of fighting men in support of a cause no one then doubted. Others were shabby, quick-buck flicks, thrown together in the grand tradition of boarding a lucrative bandwagon. On the whole, Hollywood surely did a fine job of interpreting, albeit not altogether objectively, the aims and struggles of America and her Allies in that epoch.

But Hollywood often put its best foot forward in the purely entertainment films designed to salute the millions of American boys in the service, and also to warm the hearts of the many millions more back home who felt understandably proud of their sons, husbands, and sweethearts in uniform.

The attack on Pearl Harbor which triggered U.S. entry into the war may have been a stunning surprise to Washington, but it does not seem to have caught Hollywood unprepared. The U.S. Selective Service Act, passed in September 1940, meant that close to a million boys would be in uniform within a year.

By early 1941, Hollywood was already gearing up for a spate of service-connected comedies and/or musicals. Abbott and Costello zoomed to B-Picture stardom with three films in that year, carefully chosen to give the main branches of service equal screen time: *Buck Privates, In the Navy,* and *Keep 'Em Flying.*

The same year, Bob Hope, already a top star at Paramount, appeared in *Caught in the Draft,* whose very title conveyed the dilemma of millions of young American men in 1941. Hope played a movie star who was drafted, despite all his efforts to avoid it, and had to serve his time in the Army, doing K.P., nervously donning a parachute, getting into trouble with the sergeants as well as the colonels, and making all of it hilarious.

Hope's leading lady, not surprisingly, was Dorothy Lamour, and his subordinate comedians included Lynne Overman, Eddie Bracken, Paul Hurst, and Irving Bacon. There was a dash of flag-waving, to be sure, but mostly it was good, solid comedy.

Caught in the Draft. Bob Hope played a movie star forced to report for military duty. (Paramount, 1941)

The following year, Paramount turned its attention to the Navy in *The Fleet's In* (1942), again with Dorothy Lamour as leading lady, but this time with William Holden as the sailor out to land her. (It was based, loosely, on an earlier play, "Sailor Beware.")

While it was certainly not as funny as *Caught in the Draft,* this breezy musical comedy came closer to setting the pattern for wartime musicals dealing with the boys in the service. For it was, in truth, more of a throwback to the old film revues and "follies" of the early talking era, including, as it did, a peppering of performers to toss in a song, dance, or routine whenever the plot sagged. Among them were Betty Hutton, Cass Daley, Gil Lamb, the dance team of Lorraine and Regman, and the Jimmy Dorsey Orchestra. (All of these performers,

The Fleet's In. William Holden, Dorothy Lamour, and Eddie Bracken headlined this wartime musical. (Paramount, 1942)

130

incidentally, had earlier been in-person attractions at the New York Paramount Theater during the era when big bands and subsidiary vaudeville acts were regularly featured in addition to feature films.)

Paramount went all out in name-heavy, flag-waving musicals the same year with *Star Spangled Rhythm,* in which almost everyone on the studio lot appeared. There was a story of sorts — involving sailor Eddie Bracken taking a bunch of his buddies to visit Paramount Studios, where he believes his father (Victor Moore) is a big shot, whereas Pop is only a gatekeeper.

But it was enough of an excuse for Paramount to throw in a sizable vaudeville show that included:

Paulette Goddard, Dorothy Lamour, and Veronica Lake singing "A Sweater, A Sarong, and a Peekaboo Bang." (Paulette really didn't do all that much for a sweater, but then, Lana Turner was an MGM star.)

Bob Hope and William Bendix did a sketch about jealous husbands; and Fred MacMurray, Ray Milland, Franchot Tone, and Lynne Overman did a takeoff on how women play bridge.

Vera Zorina danced to "That Old Black Magic," and Bing Crosby topped it all off with a patriotic tableau to "Old Glory."

But the Second World War was hardly a one-studio war. In 1943, Warner Brothers brought to the screen Irving Berlin's earlier Broadway success, *This is the Army,* a rousing tribute to the G.I. that one critic called "as American as hot dogs or the Bill of Rights."

Prominent in the cast were George Murphy, Joan Leslie, Alan Hale, Charles Butterworth,

Star Spangled Rhythm. **Fred MacMurray, Franchot Tone, and Ray Milland, three of the many stars in this flag-waver. (Paramount, 1942)**

This is the Army. Joan Leslie smiles for the soldiers in Irving Berlin's salute to the Army. (Warner Brothers, 1943)

Ronald Reagan, Frances Langford, and Gertrude Niesen. Plus Kate Smith, Joe Louis, and Irving Berlin, the composer singing his memorable "Oh, How I Hate to Get Up in the Morning," which he had actually introduced in a show during the First World War. To avoid charges of partiality, the film even included a number titled "Give a Cheer for the Navy," and another called "American Eagles."

And to make this worthwhile effort that much more appealing, the entire cast donated their services and Warner Brothers announced the proceeds from the movie would go to the Army Emergency Relief.

The same year, MGM made its contribution to the cause of saluting the boys with *Thousands Cheer,* a star-laden musical with a plot neither more nor less thin than the average for these

Thousands Cheer. John Boles, Gene Kelly, and Kathryn Grayson carried the thin story that motivated this big musical. (MGM, 1943)

132

wartime extravaganzas. John Boles, as an Army colonel, decides to put on an all-star show for the boys in the camp. The cast surrounding him included Gene Kelly, Kathryn Grayson, Mary Astor, and Ben Blue.

But the cast of the show he put on had Mickey Rooney, Judy Garland, Red Skelton, Eleanor Powell, Ann Sothern, Lucille Ball, Lena Horne, June Allyson, Gloria DeHaven, Jose Iturbi, and the bands of Kay Kyser, Bob Crosby, and Benny Carter.

And, in keeping with the spirit of the times, MGM held the New York opening of the movie as a bond selling event, raising some $500,000 for the U.S. Treasury.

The battle of the studios continued, each apparently determined to cram more stars into one big super-movie than its competitors. The winner was the public, which seemed more than happy to watch the steady parade of patriotic musicals telling them how great it was to have such fine boys out there defending the Four Freedoms.

By now, the message could sometimes get a bit muddy, but as long as there were a couple of dozen stars in the film and even a hint of patriotic purpose, the public was content.

Warner Brothers, unwilling to rest on its laurels after *This is the Army,* came up with another one in 1943 called *Thank Your Lucky Stars.* This one had Eddie Cantor in a dual role: as himself, boorishly trying to dominate a big all-star "benefit" show that was being prepared, and as Joe Simpson, a Hollywood tour guide who helps Dennis Morgan get a spot in the show.

But the movie had a number of treats by way of guest star specialties: Bette Davis singing "They're

Thank Your Lucky Stars. **Dennis Morgan, Joan Leslie, Eddie Cantor, and Dinah Shore front and center for the big finale. Up behind them is Alexis Smith. (Warner Brothers, 1943)**

Either Too Young Or Too Old," a wry reference to what the draft had done to the ranks of eligible and available men; John Garfield doing a tough guy's version of "Blues in the Night;" Ann Sheridan sexily singing "Love Isn't Born, It's Made;" Dinah Shore warbling the title song plus two others; and also guest stints by Errol Flynn, Jack Carson, Olivia de Havilland, Joan Leslie, Alexis Smith, Humphrey Bogart, and Spike Jones and his City Slickers.

By this time, both coasts had their famous canteens, the Stage Door Canteen in New York, and the Hollywood Canteen out West. In each place, stars were on duty every night for the benefit of visiting servicemen.

In 1943, United Artists released a film titled *Stage Door Canteen*, with Kenny Baker, Tallulah Bankhead, Ralph Bellamy, Katherine Cornell, Gracie Fields, Helen Hayes, Katharine Hepburn, Ethel Merman, Gertrude Lawrence, Ed Wynn, Ethel Waters, Lunt and Fontanne, and a few more Broadway personalities.

Hollywood could not be outdone. So, in 1944, Warner Brothers produced *Hollywood Canteen*, with a couple of dozen movie stars — from Bette Davis and John Garfield to Jack Benny and Roy Rogers.

The plot, what there was of it, was very similar to *Stage Door Canteen* — a soldier on leave visits the canteen and falls in love with a hostess.

But *Hollywood Canteen* really was a little much. Robert Hutton as the G.I. just back from the Pacific, goes through the film trying to look startled and mouthing a succession of inane lines whenever he bumps into another celebrity.

"Say, aren't you Jane Wyman?" . . . "You're Barbara Stanwyck!" . . . and "You're Mrs. Skeffington. I mean Bette Davis. I saw you on the hospital ship before you were released on the mainland."

Roy Rogers neither walks nor runs into the Hollywood Canteen. He rides in on Trigger, and, accompanied by the Sons of the Pioneers, sings "Don't Fence Me In."

Dane Clark plays the inevitable Brooklyn soldier who shows off his fractured French to Ida Lupino.

And just by luck, Hutton happens to be the one millionth G.I. to enter the Canteen, so he wins a prize — a date with Joan Leslie, with whom he is already madly in love.

(All through the Second World War, while

Hollywood Canteen. Robert Hutton and another G.I. are served by movie star John Garfield. (Warner Brothers, 1944)

Winged Victory. Don Taylor, Mark Daniels, Geraldine Wall, and Lon McCallister were in Moss Hart's tribute to the Army Air Force. (20th Century-Fox, 1944)

servicemen were proclaiming Betty Grable as their favorite pin-up, Warner Brothers kept insisting, in film after film, that Joan Leslie was the servicemen's sweetheart. With the possible exception of Miss Leslie, it is doubtful anyone was convinced.)

What Irving Berlin had done for the Army in 1943, Moss Hart did for the Army Air Corps in 1944. This was a Broadway tribute to United States airmen titled *Winged Victory*, and it was subsequently filmed by 20th Century-Fox, again with all profits destined to be turned over to Army charities.

As if to underscore its authenticity, the film's cast was made up of Hollywood actors who had

When Johnny Comes Marching Home. **Donald O'Connor, above with Peggy Ryan, pretty well reflects what Johnny planned to do after marching home. (Universal, 1943)**

actually joined the Air Corps, as well as real Air Corps personnel filling out the ranks.

The principals were Pvt. Lon McCallister, Sgt. Edmond O'Brien, Sgt. Mark Daniels, Cpl. Don Taylor, T/Sgt. Peter Lind Hayes, Cpl. Alan Baxter, Cpl. Red Buttons, Cpl. Barry Nelson, Cpl. Gary Merrill, Sgt. George Reeves, and Cpl. Karl Malden. Civilians in the cast included Jeanne Crain and Judy Holliday.

Although *Winged Victory* was not a musical (the only song used was "The Whiffenpoof Song," then very popular among Air Corps types) it was certainly a salute to the boys of the "wild blue yonder," touched with admiration and sincerity and the dramatic flair that had made Moss Hart one of the theater's most respected craftsmen.

It is interesting to note, in passing, that the unity of the nation during the Second World War seemed to extend even to the film critics who, for the most part, suspended their normal criteria and found something to praise in most of these big, splashy, wartime salutes to the boys — as if they sensed that to find and magnify minor flaws in them might be regarded as unpatriotic.

Thus far, we have dealt mostly with the "big" pictures, the major efforts of the major studios in the field of paying tribute to our boys in uniform. But the B Pictures paid their share of tributes, too.

Universal, for example, did what it could with the likes of *When Johnny Comes Marching Home* (1943), with Allan Jones as a singing marine, plus Gloria Jean, Donald O'Connor, Peggy Ryan, Jane Frazee, Phil Spitalny and his All Girl Orchestra, and the Four Step Brothers. Besides the title tune, the songs included "We Must Be Vigilant" and "This is Worth Fighting For."

Still less related to the war effort, but in keeping with the wartime notion that audiences (including the boys in uniform) wanted multi-star musicals, was the same studio's *Crazy House* (1943), an Olsen and Johnson vehicle that employed the talents of such performers as Cass Daley, Tony and Sally DeMarco, the Glenn Miller Singers (that's right), Billy Gilbert, Hans Conried, and the orchestras of Leighton Noble and Count Basie.

Columbia's *Is Everybody Happy?* (1944) had enough plot for two movies, if not enough entertainment. This one had Ted Lewis playing himself and also playing mentor to a couple of nice kids in wartime — Bob Stanford and Lynn Merrick.

The story, told in flashback, involved the younger days of Lewis and his piano-playing chum (Larry Parks) who loses an arm in the First World War and then switches to trumpet. Because of his handicap, Parks waits a long time before marrying his girl. Now, Lewis, during the Second World War, meets Parks's son (Stanford) and advises him against making the same mistake his father did — in other words, marry the girl today.

Whatever its shortcomings in the matter of sudsy story, this framework allowed lots of room for musical numbers by Lewis, Nan Wynn, Bob Haymes, and others.

Crazy House. **Olsen and Johnson and all those lovelies were just the kind of entertainment the boys in uniform loved. (Universal, 1943)**

Is Everybody Happy? Oldtimer Ted Lewis gives some advice on life to a G.I. and his girl: Bob Stanford and Lynn Merrick. (Columbia, 1944)

Republic did its bit with *Hit Parade of 1942*, which had nothing to do with the war, but cashed in on the popularity of musicals with a roster of entertainers to do their turns. Apart from the actors primarily concerned with the plot (John Carroll, Susan Hayward, Gail Patrick, and Eve Arden) the cast included Dorothy Dandridge, the Music Maids, the Golden Gate Quartet, and the bands of Count Basie, Freddy Martin, and Ray McKinley.

Columbia did much the same thing with *Jam Session* (1944), hanging a limp story on Ann Miller and Jess Barker, but tossing in the popular bands of Charlie Barnet, Louis Armstrong, Alvino Rey, Glen Gray, Teddy Powell, and Jan Garber. By way of recognizing that there was a war on, the songs included "Jive Bomber" and "Victory Polka."

Jam Session. Ann Miller was the Cinderella of this frothy yarn about a movie-struck girl. (Columbia, 1944)

Sensations of 1945. **C. Aubrey Smith presents Sophie Tucker, one of the many entertainers in this wartime show. (United Artists, 1944)**

United Artists got into the act with *Sensations of 1945* (released, typically, in mid-1944), which had a large and impressive cast, but not much else to recommend it. Among the underwhelming sensations were W.C. Fields, Sophie Tucker, Eleanor Powell, Dennis O'Keefe, Dorothy Donegan, the Les Paul Trio, and the bands of Cab Calloway and Woody Herman.

Universal came up with another one in 1944, called *Follow the Boys.* (By now, one couldn't be sure whether the boys referred to were the ones in the front lines or the ones in rival front offices.) George Raft and Vera Zorina were the stars of this sprawling musical, which was a kind of tribute to the folks of the entertainment business who devoted their time to the Hollywood Victory Committee, packaging shows for the boys in service camps and overseas.

But the cast of "specialty acts" was certainly an alluring one: Jeanette MacDonald, Dinah Shore, Orson Welles doing a magic act with Marlene Dietrich, W.C. Fields and his pool table bit, Donald O'Connor and Peggy Ryan, the Andrews Sisters,

Follow the Boys. **George Raft, Vera Zorina, and the ladies of the chorus entertain the troops. (Universal, 1944)**

Artur Rubinstein, the Delta Rhythm Boys, and the bands of Ted Lewis, Freddy Slack, Charlie Spivak, and Louis Jourdan.

By this time, it seemed as if everybody who ever had a dance band had appeared in a movie or two. Certainly it looked that way when Columbia released *Stars on Parade* (1944), with Larry Parks and Lynn Merrick. The only "stars" left to parade were the Nat King Cole Trio and the Benny Carter band.

In 1944, four Hollywood belles — Kay Francis, Carole Landis, Martha Raye, and Mitzi Mayfair — received considerable publicity through their jeep-hopping tour of U.S. service bases in England and North Africa. Naturally, an account of their adventures was filmed as *Four Jills in a Jeep,* with the original quartet of ladies playing themselves, plus Alice Faye, Carmen Miranda, Betty Grable, George Jessel, Dick Haymes, Phil Silvers, and Jimmy Dorsey and his band.

It was neither more nor less edifying than the numerous other "salutes" to our boys in uniform, but it served the purpose of providing light, inconsequential entertainment to millions of movie fans, in and out of uniform.

It has been noted, mostly in discussions about the Vietnam War, that the Second World War was the "last" war in which flag-waving songs were popular. The fact is, it was really the only U.S. war in which patriotic songs had much propaganda value. There were, of course, flag-waving songs in earlier wars, up to and including the First World War, but the combination of sound movies, the growth of radio, and the popularity of jukeboxes by the Second World War made the nationwide spreading of patriotic songs that much more efficient.

And hardly a musical film during the years of the Second World War was made that did not include at least one song aimed at either spurring our boys on to victory or bucking up the home front.

Stars on Parade. Clarence Muse, Lynn Merrick, and Larry Parks with a group of young dancers and musicians. (Columbia, 1944)

Four Jills in a Jeep. Martha Raye, Mitzi Mayfair, Kay Francis, and Carole Landis. The jeep driver is Phil Silvers. (20th Century-Fox, 1944)

Duffy's Tavern. Ed Gardner, Betty Hutton, and Victor Moore headed the all-star cast of this too-late musical. (Paramount, 1945)

Starlift. Dick Wesson is open-mouthed when Jane Wyman and Joan Leslie turn up to put on a show. (Warner Brothers, 1951)

Some of them were romantic, touching; some were clever and infectious. And some were so self-consciously "topical" as to be embarrassing. There were exceptions, but as a rule the B Pictures seemed to come up with the worst songs.

For example, *Navy Blues* (1941) included a ditty titled "When Are We Going to Land Abroad?"

True to the Army (1942) blessed us with "Whacky for Khaki."

Melody Parade (1943) saluted in music "The Woman Behind the Man Behind the Gun."

Pin-Up Girl (1944) got terribly, patriotically cute with "Red Robins, Bob Whites and Blue Birds."

And, perhaps prophetically, a ditty named "Song of the Rhineland" was introduced in a 1945 film called *Where Do We Go From Here?*

That one was issued in June of 1945, only weeks after the war in Europe had ended. Even before the war in the Pacific went into its final stages, Hollywood seemed somehow to sense that the day of saluting the boys over there was just about over, over here.

But it is probably just as difficult for studios to switch over to peacetime production as it is for defense plants. In any case, Paramount came out with one more biggie in 1945, not related to the war, but characteristic of the wartime practice of cramming many stars into one film.

This was *Duffy's Tavern*, based on the popular radio series of that time, with Ed Gardner playing Archie, as he did on the radio. With him were Victor Moore, Barry Sullivan, and Marjorie Reynolds. But the plot had something to do with Gardner and Moore reviving a recording studio, which was excuse enough to trot in all the Paramount stars for a "benefit" show, whose cast included: Bing Crosby, Betty Hutton, Paulette Goddard, Alan Ladd, Dorothy Lamour, Eddie Bracken, Sonny Tufts, Cass Daley, Barry Fitzgerald, Robert Benchley, William Demarest, Billy De Wolfe, and the four Crosby sons: Gary, Phillip, Dennis, and Lindsay. For all of that, the film was a dud.

This pretty well ended the all-star salute film. The Korean and Vietnam wars yielded a few dramas each, and none of the musical comedies that were so big in the Second World War.

There was one attempt to rally round the boys, a la Hollywood, in 1951, during the Korean War. The Warner Brothers film was called *Starlift* and dealt with entertainers going to San Francisco to do a show for Korea-bound boys. Among the stars taking part were Doris Day, Gordon MacRae, Virginia Mayo, Gene Nelson, James Cagney, Gary Cooper, Jane Wyman, Randolph Scott, Phil Harris, and Louella Parsons.

Its lack of success may be the reason that no studio tried any similar films during either the Korean or Vietnam wars. Or, more likely, those wars did not make anybody feel much like singing and celebrating.

7 Hollywood Interprets its Own

Within the limits of its own ground rules, Hollywood has long regarded biography as a fruitful garden from which to pluck ripe plots.

One of the most rigidly enforced ground rules, however, has always been that dramatic requirements must take precedence over fact. Hollywood was never noted for tolerating a factual weed in an otherwise perfectly manicured putting green of fiction.

Historical figures, both American and foreign, were natural subjects for film biography: European royalty, American presidents, frontier folk heroes, inventors, scientific pioneers, notorious outlaws, and, occasionally, artists.

No one would seriously argue that young Americans learned much truth from these film biographies, whether they dealt with Tennessee Johnson or Jesse James. But Hollywood never really perceived its function as being essentially an educational one.

Until the end of the Second World War, film biographies about show business personalities were relatively rare. Florenz Ziegfeld had been given the treatment by MGM in the 1930s. Lillian Russell had been portrayed by Alice Faye in the same decade. George M. Cohan got the full spotlight in *Yankee Doodle Dandy* (1942), impersonated by James Cagney.

But for the most part, Hollywood had stayed away from biographical movies dealing with identifiable entertainment personalities, and particularly those whose fame grew out of motion pictures.

One reason was that so many of the stars of the 1920s and 1930s were still alive and probably unwilling to be portrayed, however sympathetically, by other actors. (One thinks of Pickford, Chaplin, Garbo, Harold Lloyd and Barrymore, for instance.) And of those who were already dead (i.e., Jean Harlow, Fatty Arbuckle, Wallace Reid), their somewhat tarnished images did not always lend themselves to the kind of Horatio Alger film biographies that were deemed acceptable in that time.

But another reason may well have been that Hollywood, for all its drum-beating and chest-pounding, did not yet believe that audiences were sufficiently interested in the lives or careers of Hollywood personalities as the subjects of feature films.

An early exception was *Is Everybody Happy?* (1929), with Ted Lewis playing himself in what might be very loosely regarded as an account of his life in show business. (The title was his famous "tag" line to almost every song he performed.) But whatever the degree of truth involved in the story — and it was certainly pretty slight — the film

Is Everybody Happy? Ann Pennington seems happier than Ted Lewis in this sketchy biography of Lewis's career. (Warner Brothers, 1929)

smacked so much of the hit Al Jolson movie, *The Jazz Singer,* that the conclusion is inescapable that this picture was merely thrown together more to cash in on the dazzling success of a Jolson audible on the screen than to make any serious attempt to trace the career of Ted Lewis.

Curiously, it was Al Jolson, the harbinger of sound movies, whose life, however romanticized, sparked an epidemic of film biographies about Hollywood personalities. But it did not start until 1946.

The story behind *The Jolson Story* may well have been a better one than that purporting to be Jolson's "life" in the movie. Jolson had been a top star of both Broadway and Hollywood, but by 1946 he was fifty-eight-years-old and generally considered washed up. His string of movie musicals had fizzled out by the late 1930s, and for six years the only film appearance he made was playing himself in *Rhapsody in Blue* (1945), a fanciful biography of composer George Gershwin.

But Columbia president Harry Cohn and Hollywood columnist-turned-producer Sidney Skolsky

The Jolson Story. Larry Parks and Evelyn Keyes starred in this smash hit musical based on Jolie's life. (Columbia, 1946)

Jolson Sings Again. The sequel showed Jolson (Larry Parks again) entertaining troops in the Pacific. (Columbia, 1949)

decided to do a story loosely depicting his life. Jolson, never burdened with excessive modesty, was irked that he was not signed to play himself, but agreed to do the off-camera singing for Larry Parks, cast as Jolson. The result, however sentimental, was an $8,000,000 box-office bonanza (for those days) and led to the 1949 sequel, *Jolson Sings Again.*

It is perhaps risky to conclude that the success of *The Jolson Story* was directly responsible for the spate of film biographies of Hollywood personalities that followed in the 1950s. But Hollywood's long record of copy-catting can hardly be ignored. In the almost two decades of sound films preceding 1946 there had been only a handful of film biographies of entertainment personalities. In the decade to come there were a couple of dozen.

For example, the mid-1930s had seen the emergence of dance bands, mostly "swing" bands, as big entertainment attractions. The wartime

The Fabulous Dorseys. Janet Blair separates the bickering brothers, Tommy and Jimmy. In the background: William Lundigan. (United Artists, 1947)

143

musicals almost invariably had in their casts at least one and usually two or three bands — everyone from Xavier Cugat or Count Basie to Charlie Barnet and Spike Jones.

Even before the war, several band leaders had been used in Hollywood films: Benny Goodman in *Hollywood Hotel*, Duke Ellington in *The Hit Parade*, Louis Armstrong in *Pennies from Heaven*, plus Kay Kyser, Guy Lombardo, and several others.

But not until 1947 — the year after *The Jolson Story* — did any Hollywood studio think of a film biography of any popular band leader. The first was not terribly distinguished. It was *The Fabulous Dorseys*, with Tommy and Jimmy portraying themselves. Dragged in for guest appearances were Paul Whiteman (for whom both had worked), Charlie Barnet, Henry Busse, Ziggy Elman, Art Tatum, Bob Eberly, and Helen O'Connell. Sara Allgood and Arthur Shields played the parents of the two scrapping brothers, and apart from the numerous enjoyable musical interpolations, the movie was generally uninspired.

In 1953, Universal-International did *The Glenn Miller Story,* which turned out to be the best of the lot of film biographies based on popular band leaders. With James Stewart as Miller and June Allyson as his wife, the movie concentrated on the love story of the Millers, as well as the musician's struggle for recognition.

One thing in its favor was the meticulous reproduction of the sound of the Glenn Miller band. Another, no doubt, was the mystique about the Miller name because of his death in a plane that disappeared somewhere between England and France during the Second World War.

But there were sly touches of humor too, as when a high-ranking Air Force officer complained to Miller, after watching the band leader's uniformed band in parade, that the trombonists did not all have their slides extended an equal distance. Stewart (Miller) could not quite bring himself to explain that they were playing different notes.

Two years later, Universal-International reasoned that if Glenn Miller was worth a movie, surely Benny Goodman, "the king of swing," was. As in the Miller film, the music was authentic (former sidemen Gene Krupa, Teddy Wilson, and Lionel Hampton played themselves), and Steve Allen, cast as Goodman, even took clarinet lessons so he could appear to be playing Goodman's

The Glenn Miller Story. Charles Drake, Steve Pendleton, and James Stewart. Among other things, Miller's music was faithfully duplicated. (U-I, 1953)

musical solos. (The music was actually played by Goodman.)

But the script was pretty lifeless, there apparently being little usable drama in Goodman's life story, and Allen, an intelligent, witty, jazz-oriented television personality, lacked the range as an actor to make Goodman seem even mildly compelling.

The *Gene Krupa Story* (1959) was a shade better, partly because Sal Mineo, nobody's favorite actor, gave a fairly convincing portrayal as Krupa, and mostly because it had a message, of sorts.

Krupa's periodic troubles with police and border authorities arising out of possession of narcotics were well enough publicized that no movie about him could very well ignore them. So the facts (dressed up, no doubt) were used as part of the story, Krupa being depicted as a reckless young man who made a mistake and learned his lesson. However whitewashed, this at least gave the story some dramatic direction.

Musically, the film was on surer ground. Krupa provided the actual drum work, but Mineo worked hard at duplicating his movements. And such musicians as Red Nichols, Shelly Manne, Anita O'Day, and Bobby Troup added worthwhile contributions.

These jazzmen who were the subjects of Hollywood film biographies — the Dorseys, Miller, Goodman, Krupa, and Red Nichols in Danny Kaye's *The Five Pennies* (1959) — were not truly moviemade celebrities, although all had been featured in some movies.

To some extent, too, some of them followed the

The Benny Goodman Story. That's Steve Allen pretending to play the clarinet, as Benny Goodman. (U-I, 1955)

The Gene Krupa Story. Sal Mineo, as the famous drummer, did time behind bars for smoking pot. (Columbia, 1959)

lead of *The Jolson Story* in another respect. Jolson was portrayed as a pioneer among popular entertainers, sticking doggedly to his "new" way of singing, despite opposition from veteran entrepreneurs, until the public accepted it. Similarly, Miller and Goodman were both shown as struggling against ignorant band bookers, stubbornly playing their music in their own way until the public accepted it and made them stars. Whatever truth there was in this approach — and it would seem to apply more to Goodman than the others — it was a handy dramatic device, certainly not new to Hollywood but usable in "biographies" of musical artists. It tended to put Goodman and Miller in the same class with Louis Pasteur and Madame Curie.

Pioneers in any field make good movie heroes, and the most unlikely historical figures have been so cloaked to make them better conform to Hollywood's theory of what the public could grasp.

Hollywood has also, now and then, paid tribute to America's songwriters, frequently emphasizing that the hero of the particular biography wrote songs that were "different." Hollywood films have

Three Little Words. **Red Skelton, Vera-Ellen and Fred Astaire were in this story about two songwriters. (MGM, 1950)**

saluted George Gershwin *(Rhapsody in Blue)*, Cole Porter *(Night and Day)*, Jerome Kern *(Till the Clouds Roll By)*, Rodgers and Hart *(Words and Music)*, Sigmund Romberg *(Deep In My Heart)*, and such others as Victor Herbert and Stephen Foster. But most of these were merely excuses to lump together the songs of each composer and have them performed, with appropriately lavish surroundings, by well-known entertainers.

There were a few other film biographies of songwriters, lesser known perhaps, but somewhat more germaine to the Hollywood scene. This is not to say they were any more authentic as biographies, but they dealt, at least in part, with the careers of songwriters in Hollywood.

First there was *Three Little Words* (1950), a rather unpretentious musical with Fred Astaire as Bert Kalmar and Red Skelton as Harry Ruby.

Besides the title tune, Kalmar and Ruby wrote many hits during the years of their collaboration, and the film featured a number of them. Besides their work on Broadway, they provided some of the songs for films with the Marx Brothers, Eddie Cantor, Wheeler and Woolsey, Dick Powell, and others.

Dramatically, *Three Little Words* touched some of the ups and downs of their careers, including a misunderstanding that separated them for a time. What made it unusual as musicals go was that both Astaire and Skelton were relatively subdued, paying some attention to the characters rather than simply doing dance and comedy routines, respectively.

In 1951, Warner Brothers saluted Gus Kahn, a veteran lyricist who collaborated with, among others, George Gershwin, Isham Jones, Walter Donaldson, Harry Warren, Jimmy McHugh, Vincent Youmans, Ted Fiorito, and Sigmund Romberg. The film was titled *I'll See You in my Dreams,* after a Kahn lyric, and had Danny Thomas in the leading role.

It traced his life and career — with what degree of accuracy, one hesitates to guess — through Tin Pan Alley, Broadway and Hollywood, with Doris Day as the young girl he married, and Frank Lovejoy playing composer Walter Donaldson. It was hokey, sentimental, and not notably original, but Thomas's engaging manner made Kahn interesting and, of course, the songs made it entertaining.

Better still was *The Best Things in Life are Free* (1956), again taking its title from a song written by the film's leading characters, in this case a trio: Buddy DeSylva (played by Gordon MacRae), Ray Henderson (Dan Dailey), and Lew Brown (Ernest Borgnine).

Again, it was the old climb up the ladder of success, from Tin Pan Alley to Hollywood. Again, there was the team splitting up after an argument, but not for long.

What carried the film were the songs, plus the easy playing of the three stars. And as a bonus there was Sheree North, looking delectable and dancing quite capably in a couple of eye-filling production numbers.

But the movie biographies of songwriters and band leaders, entertaining though some of them may have been, were not the main result of the success of *The Jolson Story.* After 1946, Hollywood really began to look into its own files, digging up subjects for possible film biographies of people really associated with Hollywood. And they found quite a few.

An obvious choice was Pearl White, the queen of the silent serials. A onetime circus performer who could do her own stunt work, she became famous

I'll See You in My Dreams. Patrice Wymore clings to Danny Thomas, whose songwriting partner was Frank Lovejoy, at the keyboard. (Warner Brothers, 1951)

The Best Things in Life Are Free. Gordon MacRae was one of a songwriting trio in this entertaining film. (20th Century-Fox, 1956)

The Perils of Pauline. Billy De Wolfe menaces Betty Hutton in this scene from the movie more or less about Pearl White. (Paramount, 1947)

Valentino. Anthony Dexter's appearance came closer to Rudolph Valentino than anything else in the movie. (Columbia, 1951)

in *The Perils of Pauline,* a 1914 serial crammed with thrills and narrow escapes. This was followed by *The Exploits of Elaine,* which was more of the same. (Happily, Miss White then switched to features, else we might have been assailed with an array of alliterative adventures: *The Dangers of Diane, The Jeopardy of Judy, The Hazards of Hazel,* right down to *The Zounds of Zelda.*) But Miss White's enduring identity remained that of Pauline, heroine of scores of brushes with death.

In 1947, Paramount brought out a film called *The Perils of Pauline,* which was neither a continuation of the old serial nor an authentic biography of Pearl White, but a little bit of each. Betty Hutton played Miss White, somewhat as if she thought the studio was on fire, and the movie took a tongue-in-cheek approach to its subject, including the filming of an oldtime "chase," but allowing Miss Hutton to be her buoyant self rather than Pearl White.

Besides Betty, the cast had John Lund, Billy De Wolfe, and William Demarest, plus such veteran pie-hurlers as Chester Conklin, James Finlayson, and Hank Mann.

Whatever its imperfections as biography, *The Perils of Pauline* offered fun galore, including a complicated sequence in which four quickie movies were being filmed simultaneously on a subdivided set: a jungle adventure, a Western, a drama, and a comedy.

Another silent era superstar whose brilliant career cried out for film biography was Rudolph Valentino, the greatest romantic leading man the

148

movies have ever produced. Columbia tackled the subject in 1951, but it was at best a flying tackle that missed.

Valentino was the title, Anthony Dexter played the title role, and Eleanor Parker played the one and only lady love in his smouldering life. Apart from Dexter's passable resemblance to Valentino, nothing in the movie came close, either to the facts or to an acceptable fictionalization of Valentino's life. (Irving Shulman's smutty biography of Valentino had not yet been published.) The movie was pure soap opera from start to finish, and neither the approximation of the fashions and filmmaking techniques of the era nor the shallow interpretations of the people in it did anything to make it memorable.

Nine years later, in 1960, a documentary feature called *The Legend of Valentino* proved rather more acceptable, including, as it did, numerous clips from Valentino's most famous movies and at least an orderly narrative of the highlights of his spectacular career. If Valentino remained an enigmatic figure at the end of it, at least that is closer to the truth; the sloppily embroidered fiction in the 1951 "biography" was far less believable.

The Legend of Valentino. **The real McCoy was seen in this documentary, made up mostly of clips from his films. (Walter Reade, 1960)**

Yet another Hollywood giant was eulogized in *The Story of Will Rogers* (1952), with Will Rogers, Jr. playing his world-famous father. The script was based on the reminiscences of Rogers's widow, and it was marked by affection and relatively little drama.

The younger Rogers was moderately successful in suggesting the manner and personality of his father, Jane Wyman was the personification of wifely loyalty as Mrs. Rogers, and Carl Benton Reid played Roger's father, a presumably cantankerous old type who kept insisting Will would never amount to anything.

(It seems axiomatic that no film biography of any famous person can ever be made without the presence of some relative or in-law harrumphing his way through the script, regularly predicting that the hero will never amount to anything. The only exception that comes to mind was *The King of Kings.*)

For show biz flavor *The Story of Will Rogers* had William Forrest as Florenz Ziegfeld, and Eddie Cantor, a Ziegfeld Follies contemporary of Will's, playing himself.

It was not an especially penetrating biography, but it succeeded at least in evoking, through Rogers's own sayings and his son's affectionate portrayal, the flavor of the man it saluted.

In what appeared to be a straight player deal, Will Rogers, Jr. returned the favor Eddie Cantor did him by appearing as Will Rogers in *The Eddie Cantor Story* (1953), also from Warners, and produced by Sidney Skolsky, who more or less began the movie star biography syndrome with *The Jolson Story.*

But except for a brief appearance at the end of the film, Eddie Cantor did not play Eddie Cantor. This task was assigned to Keefe Brasselle, a sort of latter-day Sonny Tufts, who tried very hard to imitate the visual trademarks of Cantor — rolling eyes, flapping hands, simple dance steps — and succeeded only in suggesting a night club impressionist's caricature. The singing, as in the Jolson films, was done off-camera by the subject of the biography.

The story was, understandably, about the long and happy love of Eddie and his Ida (played by Marilyn Erskine), and touched on some of the triumphs of the Cantor career. It also featured a good many of the songs Cantor popularized.

In between Will Rogers and Eddie Cantor came

The Story of Will Rogers. Eddie Cantor played himself and Will Rogers, Jr., played his famed father. (Warner Brothers, 1952)

The Eddie Cantor Story. Keefe Brasselle played Cantor, but Eddie supplied the off-camera singing. (Warner Brothers, 1953)

150

Jane Froman, the subject of a big and handsome film biography called *With a Song in my Heart* (1952). Although Miss Froman was not essentially a film star, she did appear in a few movies in the 1930s and, of course, was more widely known through radio, night clubs, and theater.

Unlike some of the film biogs mentioned, Miss Froman's life included a dramatic incident which, properly handled, gave the story a sense of direction. She was crippled in an airplane crash in 1943 and this tragedy was utilized to demonstrate the singer's courage and determination in rebuilding her career. The role was played with brassy gumption by Susan Hayward.

David Wayne played Miss Froman's husband, a man not too happy at being the husband of a star. Rory Calhoun played the pilot who rescued her after the crash and became her new amour. And, in keeping with the Jolson-Cantor technique, the singing apparently done by Susan Hayward was actually performed by Jane Froman.

In 1953, Hollywood paid tribute to another early star, Grace Moore, who was best known as a star of opera but also became a popular film star in the early 1930s. The movie was called *So This is Love* and had Kathryn Grayson as Miss Moore. The singer's dedication to her career provided the main thrust of this movie, tracing the struggles she overcame in her fight for recognition. Along the way, according to this gospel, she was offered love and marriage twice, first by a young man played by Merv Griffin, and later by one portrayed by Douglas Dick. But the singer would not be side-tracked from her burning ambition to sing at the Met, and if it seems a hollow victory when she realizes this ambition, we are given to understand that was the way Grace Moore wanted it. Since the film claimed to have been based on her own autobiography, one can only assume there must have been something to all this. In any case, Kathryn Grayson did the best she could with this story and also sang any number of solos presumably from the repertoire of the late opera and sometime movie star.

In 1956 came the first of what might be termed the combination biography-cum-exposé movies. It was called *I'll Cry Tomorrow,* dealt with the bumpy career of singer Lillian Roth, and starred that intrepid nonsinging portrayer of singers, Susan Hayward.

Miss Roth, a nightclub and Broadway theater star, had appeared in several films in the early 1930s, but was long since forgotten when first a book about her and then this film biography appeared.

Unlike the standard climbing-the-ladder-of-success approach to most show business film biographies, *I'll Cry Tomorrow* offered us a rather pathetic figure, a shy young girl driven by her ambitious mother (Jo Van Fleet) into a singing career she never really wanted.

When Mama breaks up her romance with lawyer Ray Danton, Lillian broods. Danton dies in a hospital and Lillian goes on singing. But soon she takes to drink, which gives her more confidence in her performing, but also gets her into bad company. She meets playboy Don Taylor and the two of them go on a drinking spree. They awake (in twin beds and fully clothed) to find they are married.

Next, Lillian meets Richard Conte, who turns out to be a reformed alcoholic and something of a sadist, and Lillian Roth's plunge into obscurity continues.

With a Song in My Heart. **Susan Hayward portrayed singer Jane Froman. The young G.I. is Robert Wagner. (20th Century-Fox, 1952)**

So This is Love. Impersonating Grace Moore was Kathryn Grayson, above, with Merv Griffin. (Warner Brothers, 1953)

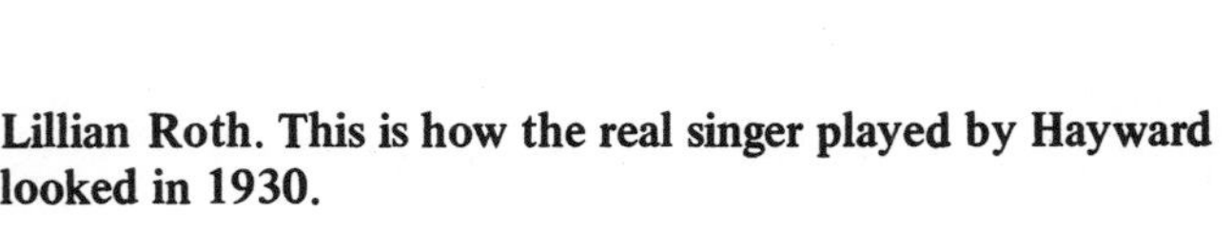

I'll Cry Tomorrow. Susan Hayward survived a stage mother, some rocky romances and alcoholism. At the piano is Eddie Albert. (MGM, 1956)

Lillian Roth. This is how the real singer played by Hayward looked in 1930.

The solution, such as it is, comes when she meets kindly Eddie Albert at an Alcoholics Anonymous meeting, and eventually learns she can sing and enjoy it, without a few drinks under her belt.

If *I'll Cry Tomorrow* tended to get rather preachy toward the end — a common pitfall for films concerning the work of AA — it at least gave us a film biography of a Hollywood performer that had more depth than the usual peaches-and-cream stories built around Cantor, Rogers, Valentino, and others. And Miss Hayward's performance won her an Oscar nomination.

Even before the Lillian Roth opus, Hollywood was having a look at another singer of the 1920s and 1930s. She was Ruth Etting, and like Roth she was primarily known through her work in nightclubs, theater, and radio; but she, too, had made several films. In 1955, MGM released *Love Me or Leave Me,* with Doris Day as Ruth Etting and James Cagney as Martin Snyder, the hoodlum in her past who will not stop interfering with her future.

Some of this, at least, was based on fact and it served as a better-than-average story line for a musical biography of a once popular singer. For Cagney, the role of the feisty Snyder was just another in a long string of powerful performances. For Miss Day, it was probably the best role of her movie career and she proved to be up to it. Late in the movie, "Gimp" Snyder decided to reassert himself by becoming a movie producer, once again taking over Ruth's career, and behaving no more boorishly than, one suspects, other producers of similarly shady beginnings have occasionally behaved.

There were, naturally, a collection of Miss Etting's hits to be sung, and Doris handled these with her customary polish. Rounding out the cast

Love Me or Leave Me. **Doris Day was Ruth Etting and James Cagney played the hoodlum in her life. (MGM, 1955)**

were Cameron Mitchell, Robert Keith, and Tom Tully.

In 1957, Warners tried to do right by Helen Morgan, perhaps the greatest "torch" singer of her time. But the film, *The Helen Morgan Story*, did not even come close to the mark.

To begin with, they cast the fragile, sweet Ann Blyth as Helen Morgan, thus missing the chance for any emotional depth one had a right to expect from the earthy character. One would assume Miss Blyth got the role partly because she was a singer — although of a somewhat different stripe — but no, she did not even do her own singing. For that, the voice of Gogi Grant was used, and she came closer to approaching the husky, melancholy style of Morgan.

(Coincidentally, the same year, CBS did a television special called *The Helen Morgan Story*, with Polly Bergen in the role. Miss Bergen did both her own singing and her own acting and, on the whole, left both Blyth and Grant at the starting gate.)

Among those to whom the movie Miss Morgan gave pieces of her breaking heart were Paul Newman and Richard Carlson, and, for a touch of atmosphere, the movie also employed Rudy Vallee, Walter Winchell, and songwriter Jimmy McHugh, all playing themselves. But it was all to no avail. Even perched on a piano, Miss Blyth looked as if she were about to sell a Twinkie.

But Hollywood was not through paying lavish, if inaccurate, tributes to its veterans, living or dead.

Having already covered (in film, if not with glory) Valentino, Will Rogers, Pearl White, Al Jolson, and Eddie Cantor, there were still some to go.

One who yielded a reasonably good film biography was Lon Chaney, in Universal's *Man of a Thousand Faces* (1957), with James Cagney essaying the Chaney part.

This one had some built-in dramatic elements that gave it a running start. Chaney's parents were deaf and mute, and his early training in communicating with them served him well later in mastering the arts of pantomime.

Cagney, subduing as much as possible his pugnacious side, tried to make Chaney a sensitive, sympathetic man, loyal to his parents, infinitely patient with a first wife (Dorothy Malone) who defied understanding. For the most part he succeeded. Even more fascinating was Cagney's

The Helen Morgan Story. Striking the familiar Morgan pose (atop a piano) is Ann Blyth, in the title role. (Warner Brothers, 1957)

Man of a Thousand Faces. James Cagney played Lon Chaney. The two women in his life are Dorothy Malone and Jane Greer. (U-I, 1957)

duplication of the famous Chaney disguises (for *The Phantom of the Opera* and *The Hunchback of Notre Dame*), and the film's convincing reproduction of the aura of the silent film studios.

But what is one to say of *Jeanne Eagels* (1957), the movie supposedly based on that once famous actress's life? Jeanne Eagels was first a Broadway star, best remembered, perhaps, as Sadie Thompson in "Rain." But she did make some films in the late 1920s. And it is generally known that she had a good bit of trouble with the bottle and with a succession of men.

Throwing common sense to the winds, Columbia chose to play this role Kim Novak, of whom one pitiless critic once remarked: "She couldn't act wet in a flood." And, as if admitting that she needed all the help she could get, the studio glossed over most of the facts of Miss Eagels's life, substituting instead a parade of clichés so banal as to make one almost sympathize with Miss Novak.

Accessories after the fact included Jeff Chandler, as a carnival man who first discovers Jeanne, Charles Drake as a college man who later joins her in matrimony as well as in drinking, and Agnes Moorehead as a drama coach, burdened with the movie's least believable line: "This girl has talent!"

In the same year, Paramount decided it was time to salute Buster Keaton, one of the titans of silent screen comedy. Keaton himself served as technical adviser for the movie, which was called, with stunning originality, *The Buster Keaton Story.* Donald O'Connor was chosen to play Keaton.

This one and some of the earlier film biographies point up a curious fact about movies depicting the lives of famous entertainers: it appears to be less difficult to find actors who can convincingly re-create the personalities, and more or less duplicate the theatrical styles of such stars, than to come up with soundly structured biographies of the stars' lives.

Jeanne Eagels. **Kim Novak, in the title role, fought the battle of the bottle and lost. Above, right: Charles Drake. (Columbia, 1957)**

It is tempting to place the blame on the moviemakers and their long-famous low opinion of the public's intelligence. Time and again, there has been ample evidence that the facts of anyone's life were not regarded by the filmmakers as sufficiently dramatic to hold an audience's attention. That may sometimes have been a valid point, but the trouble is that too often the "biographies" that were concocted to shore up the sagging facts were not only not better but substantially worse.

In any case, Donald O'Connor made a rather good Buster Keaton, in terms of studying and then imitating the marvelously inventive comedy routines that had made Keaton such a big star of silent films. O'Connor's own fluidity, his great skill as a comic dancer, were certainly strong assets in his attempt to capture the essence of Keaton's fumbling, uncertain manner, and adroit appearance of awkwardness.

But as to the script, it was once again a tower of mush, with Keaton depicted as a man who goes to pieces after he is spurned by an ambitious movie queen (Rhonda Fleming) and is later saved by the love of a long-suffering casting director (Ann Blyth). Peter Lorre, Larry Keating, and Richard Anderson played supporting roles.

All things considered, it might have been better had Keaton served not only as a technical adviser on the style of his comedy but also as an expert witness on the facts of his own life.

In the mid-1950s, James Dean became a movie star, seemingly overnight, and a particular favorite with the younger fans. After studying at the famed Actors Studio in New York, Dean launched what looked as if it might become an important Broadway career. But Hollywood beckoned and he went West to appear in *East of Eden* (1955). Acclaimed for his brooding portrayal of Raymond Massey's unloved son, he was promptly cast in *Rebel Without a Cause* (1955) and rapidly became the symbol of discontented youth.

Next came *Giant* (1956), a sprawling George Stevens production based on the Edna Ferber book. But before it was released, James Dean's rapid rise to stardom was brutally snapped in an automobile accident that took his life.

But the Dean cult survived and grew, and in 1957 Warner Brothers, where he had made all three of his pictures, strung together a documentary called *The James Dean Story.* Narrated by Martin Gabel and featuring brief appearances by some of

The Buster Keaton Story. Donald O'Connor, Rhonda Fleming, and Ivan Triesault. O'Connor made a good Keaton, but the script was leaky. (Paramount, 1957)

The James Dean Story. This documentary traced the brief career of Dean, seen above in his racing car. (Warner Brothers, 1957)

the people who knew him, plus some clips from his recorded work, it was an elegiac tribute to a young man whose brief career (and, no doubt, his early death) made him a hero to a generation who saw themselves in him, or, at any rate, in the title of one of his films — *Rebel Without a Cause.*

(The Dean cult got another boost or two almost twenty years later. NBC Television came up with a new documentary film titled *James Dean, Portrait of a Friend,* with Stephen McHattie as the enigmatic young actor. This was based on a book, *James Dean: A Biography,* by William Bast, who had been Dean's roommate at UCLA in 1950. Released to theaters the same year, 1976, was yet another feature called *James Dean: The First American Teenager.* In this one, documentarian Ray Connolly persuaded such film personalities as Dennis Hopper, Natalie Wood, and Sal Mineo to talk about Dean. Once again, excerpted scenes from Dean's few screen performances were included.)

Warner Brothers issued yet another film biography in 1958, this one based on Diana Barrymore's somewhat sensational autobiography, *Too Much, Too Soon*. Diana, the daughter of John Barrymore, had worked both on stage and screen, but succumbed, it seemed, to booze and thus destroyed what might have been a promising career. She wrote her book in collaboration with Gerold Frank, an old hand at hearing the confessions of dried-out drinkers, having earlier worked with Lillian Roth on *I'll Cry Tomorrow*. Frank and Miss Barrymore were fairly candid in their book, but much of this was toned down — or cleaned up — for the movie.

What was left was a fairly good performance by Dorothy Malone as Diana, and a rather splendid one by Errol Flynn as her famous father. The men in her life, all more or less whitewashed, were played by Efrem Zimbalist, Jr., Ray Danton, and Edward Klemmer. But neither the script nor the direction gave them much help.

Ray Danton got a much better break three years later playing the title role in *The George Raft Story*, which traced (rather shakily) that dancer-actor's rise from the speakeasy to the silver screen. Raft, according to the movie, was just too nice a guy, unable to turn his back on old chums, even if they were hoodlums, and therefore suffered career setbacks.

The cast of this Allied Artists effort was interesting enough. There was dancer Barrie Chase, as a nice young dancer; Barbara Nichols as Texas Guinan; Jayne Mansfield as a blonde who hangs around Raft's house; and "guest star" Neville Brand as Al Capone.

One of the film's more interesting scenes concerned the time soon after Raft won considerable notice as a coin-flipping hood in *Scarface*, in which Paul Muni starred as a character widely regarded as being based on Capone. Raft, in Chicago for a personal appearance, is taken forcibly by a couple of plug-uglies to the posh office of Capone (Brand), who seems annoyed at the movie presumably based on him. But Raft (Danton) sweet-talks the Big Guy and Capone finally admits he was only annoyed at the Hays Office for bumping him off in the movie.

This incident is also related in a recent (1975) biography of George Raft written by Lewis Yablonsky. But curiously, newspaper clippings and reference books indicate that Capone was already in jail (serving an eleven-year sentence for income tax evasion) some six months *before Scarface* was released, in May 1932.

(In his own autobiography, *"A Child of the Century,"* Ben Hecht, who wrote the script for *Scarface*, tells of being visited in Hollywood by two Capone henchmen, after he had written the script but before the film was shot. He pacified them, Hecht recalled, by assuring them the movie was not to be about Al Capone. If the Raft-Capone meeting as related in the film really did take place, it would seem Capone did not remain mollified by Hecht's glib invention.)

At any rate, *The George Raft Story* was a cut above some of the film biographies — despite some questionable incidents — at least partly because Raft apparently had no objection to the inclusion of his early underworld connections.

In 1962, Marilyn Monroe died and her home studio, 20th Century-Fox, did not wait a year before releasing *Marilyn*, a documentary biographical film featuring clips from some fifteen of her movies, with connecting narration by Rock Hudson. It was, logically, an affectionate tribute, despite the fact that she had had her clashes with the heads of the studio, and if it did little to enlighten us as to what manner of woman Marilyn Monroe had been, it at least recalled some highlights of her film career.

(The Monroe cult was to continue for a good many years, resulting in numerous books on her, a couple of television tributes, and yet more attention from Hollywood.)

In 1965 came the battle of the *Harlows*. It started when Irving Shulman wrote a steamy biography of Jean Harlow, the movies' sex queen of the 1930s, which quickly became a best-seller. Latter-day movie mogul Joseph E. Levine, never one to let a good prospect go by, bought the screen rights to the book and undertook to produce what was to be one of the biggies of the year.

But somebody beat him to the draw. Using a quickie filming system called Electronovision, the Magna Distribution Corporation managed to get their *Harlow* out in May 1965, just two months ahead of Levine's effort for Paramount.

As things turned out, it was a race to a pointless finish line. The first of the two films had Carol Lynley as Harlow, Ginger Rogers as her mother, Jack Kruschen as Louis B. Mayer, Hurd Hatfield as Paul Bern, Harlow's husband who killed himself, and even Hermione Baddeley as Marie Dressler. It

Too Much, Too Soon. Dorothy Malone played Diana Barrymore, and Errol Flynn was her father, John Barrymore. (Warner Brothers, 1958)

158

The George Raft Story. Ray Danton, left, played Raft in this fairly candid biography of the actor-dancer's career. (Allied Artists, 1961)

Marilyn. This documentary about Marilyn Monroe, made less than a year after her death, included numerous clips from her films. (20th Century-Fox, 1963)

also had a stupefyingly dull script, and looked exactly like what it was — an inept quickie.

The second *Harlow* was a cut above it, but only just. This one had Carroll Baker as Jean Harlow, which in itself was no particular improvement over Miss Lynley. It also had Angela Lansbury as Jean's mother, Peter Lawford as Paul Bern, Martin Balsam as a character based on (but not identified as) Louis B. Mayer, and Red Buttons as the loyal agent who discovered Jean and helped her to stardom.

But even *Harlow* number two, based on Shulman's book, shied away from some of the revelations that had made the book so successful — possibly fearing censorship problems, libel suits, or both.

So, in the end, we got two Harlow movies, barely two months apart, and both merely routine additions to the long list of watered-down film biographies, no more revealing of what the subject of the biography was really like, no more imaginative in avoiding the lengthy roster of film biography clichés, no more original in their respective approaches to film biography than had been the soapy salutes to Helen Morgan, Eddie Cantor, or Valentino.

And in 1968, the career of Gertrude Lawrence was superficially examined in *Star!*, with Julie Andrews as Miss Lawrence. It was a sumptuous, three-hour feast of musical production numbers and re-created scenes from Lawrence vehicles, but Miss Andrews was still a little too Mary Poppinsish to suggest the sophistication, glamor, or wit that made Gertrude Lawrence such an international favorite during her lifetime.

Supporting Miss Andrews were Richard Crenna as her husband and Daniel Massey as Noel Coward, but even their efforts, plus all that energetic singing and prancing from Miss Julie, could not keep *Star!* from being the box-office flop that it was.

Earlier the same year, William Wyler, one of Hollywood's finest directors, turned his attention to the Barbra Streisand vehicle, *Funny Girl*, which had made her a Broadway star. Based roughly on the early career of Fanny Brice, it was a splendid showcase for Streisand's peculiar charms, and Wyler's production was both handsome and entertaining. But, as usual, some facts got lost in the shuffle. Omar Sharif, as her knight errant, was decidedly fictioned up.

In 1972, director Sidney J. Furie gave us an erratic biography of the great blues singer, Billie Holiday, titled *Lady Sings the Blues.* The movie swung wildly from vivifying some of the sordid facts of Lady Day's life to hopelessly romanticizing others. Yet, Diana Ross, in the title role, somehow managed to be both appealing and convincing, perhaps most of all in her imitation of the look and sound of Billie.

The box-office success of *Funny Girl* led, as such things always do, to a sequel in 1975 called *Funny Lady,* which claimed to take up Fanny Brice's later adventures. Nicky Arnstein (Sharif again, in a brief appearance) gets his walking papers from Fanny, who later meets and falls for Billy Rose (played by James Caan) who later leaves Fanny for swimmer Eleanor Holm. Besides some highly entertaining musical numbers, *Funny Lady* offered a slightly subdued Streisand, suggesting the

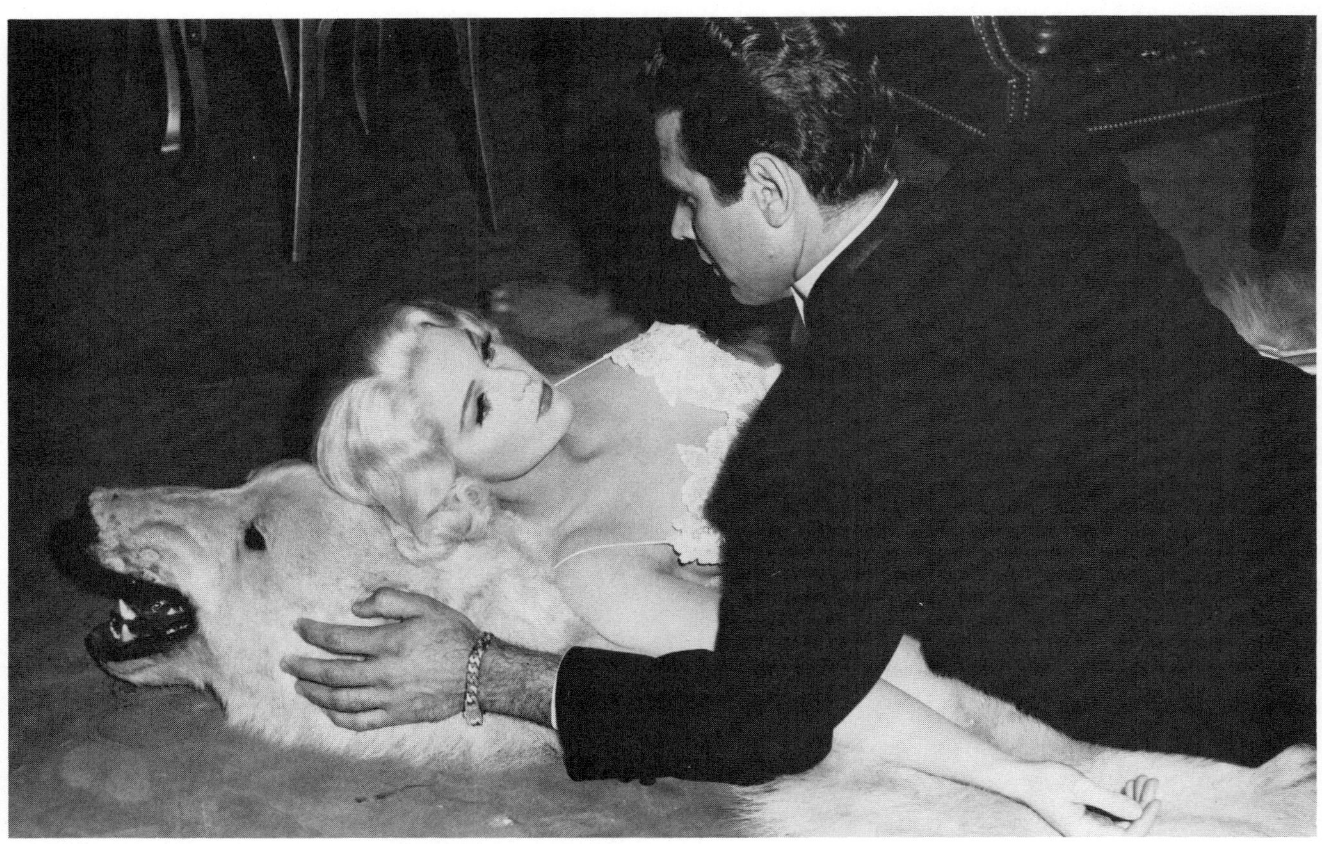

Harlow. Carol Lynley and Michael Dante in the first (quickie) of the biographies of Jean Harlow. (Magna, 1965)

Harlow. Carroll Baker was Jean Harlow this time, seen here with Peter Lawford and Michael Connors. (Paramount, 1965)

Star. Julie Andrews played Gertrude Lawrence and Daniel Massey was Noel Coward. (20th Century-Fox, 1968)

maturing Brice, and a winning performance by Caan, despite the fact that he is about twice the height and weight of the pint-sized Billy Rose.

Watching *Funny Lady,* one gets the feeling that Ms. Streisand had memorized the script before Caan was assigned the role of Billy Rose. She repeatedly refers to him as "that little shrimp" or "that little jerk," blissfully ignoring the fact that he towers over her — as, in fact, Rose had not towered over Fanny Brice. Perhaps it was an attempt at making Caan *seem* smaller, but the visual evidence to the contrary is too overpowering for such a ploy to work.

For all the time, money, effort, and film expended on these numerous biographies of stars, Hollywood rarely turned out one that could be called truly memorable.

One reason for this has been the filmmakers' cavalier disregard for fact. They thought no more of turning a hood into a hero than of eliminating a

Funny Girl. Barbra Streisand was a good Fanny Brice and Omar Sharif was a too-good Nicky Arnstein. (Columbia, 1968)

161

Lady Sings the Blues. **Diana Ross played Billie Holliday in this biopic about the great jazz singer. (Paramount, 1972)**

Funny Lady. **The further adventures of Fanny Brice, with Barbra Streisand again and James Caan, at piano, as Billy Rose. (Columbia, 1975)**

husband or two from the shadowy past of this or that glamor queen.

But more than that, the problem has usually been Hollywood's insistence on formula films, in which heroes must be flawlessly heroic, villains villainous, and fallen stars simply the victims of cruel fate.

Whether the movie was about war, peace, love, hate, greed, fear, or the life of a movie star, Hollywood's film factories seemed incapable of escaping the web of clichés they had woven, nurtured, and come to believe in.

As to the film biographies, truth may have been both stranger and more entertaining than fiction, but Hollywood rarely let audiences judge that for themselves.

8 Hollywood Recycles its Gold

Although the word recycling is relatively new, the practice has been going on for some years, ever since certain industries figured out a way of reusing materials that had become run down but not destroyed — as in scrap iron, auto tires, bottles, beer cans, and paper.

Hollywood more or less tripped over the theory, if not the word, some thirty years ago. In 1946, Bing Crosby and Bob Hope had already made four of their famous "Road" pictures, and all had met with great popular success and even some grudging critical approval.

One would think that any movie with the word "road" in the title and Crosby (though not Hope) in the cast would draw crowds. So, in 1946, a company called Astor released a feature-length film starring Bing Crosby and cunningly titled *The Road to Hollywood*. But it had nothing at all to do with the highly salable Crosby-Hope series of films. Instead, it was a paste-up of four Mack Sennett shorts Crosby had made back in 1930, when he was not quite big enough a name for feature films.

These shorts included a Crosby song or two and many recycled Sennett gags that he had previously used in his Keystone Cops era. The shorts were titled "Billboard Girl," "Dream House," "I Surrender Dear," and "One More Chance," the last two capitalizing on then current Crosby hits. Each ran about twenty minutes, thus making a "feature" of eighty minutes. But the public did not really fall for this shell game, and *The Road to Hollywood* quickly vanished into that limbo of forgotten films that seemed like good ideas at the time.

But the theory of recycling did not. Three years later (1949) Eagle Lion, the British company, got hold of some old Sennett reels and put them together into a feature called *Down Memory Lane*. (At least this title was closer to the truth.) The original cast — that is, those in the Sennett shorts that provided the meat for this feature — included Crosby again, plus Gloria Swanson, W.C. Fields, Ben Turpin, the Keystone Cops, and the Sennett Bathing Beauties. Director Phil Karlson was shrewd enough to include some new footage: TV host Steve Allen deciding to show his viewers some old movies. He also tossed in the services of veteran comic actors Franklin Pangborn and Frank Nelson. The result was a bit more acceptable than *The Road to Hollywood*, but the box-office success of *Down Memory Lane* was negligible.

No doubt, the emergence of television had a good deal to do with the first wave of movie nostalgia that swept across America in the late 1940s and early 1950s. That insatiable devourer of product found it had to rely on old movies to fill in the hours between live — and far more expensive

The Road to Hollywood. Timed to cash in on the famous "Road" pictures, this was a compilation of early Crosby shorts. (Astor, 1946)

Down Memory Lane. The same compilation included another early Bing Crosby short made for Sennett. (Eagle Lion, 1949)

Down Memory Lane. Chester Conklin and some Mack Sennett Bathing Beauties. (Eagle Lion, 1949)

— programs. Thus, a whole new generation of youngsters discovered W.C. Fields, Laurel and Hardy, and other old favorites of earlier generations. And the receding hairline set could wallow in nostalgia in the wee hours, looking again at the antics of comics long since considered passé.

In time, Hollywood sensed this growing interest in the films of yesteryear, particularly those starring comedians no longer active, and decided to cash in on it.

Abbott and Costello, then still riding high as a comedy team, romped through a look-back at early Hollywood in *Abbott and Costello Meet the Keystone Kops* (1955), with Fred Clark as a double-dealing producer and a cast that even had Mack Sennett as himself. Strictly speaking, this was not recycling so much as re-creating, but it helped pave the way for other, more notable, gift-wrapped oldies. And, in their own broadly slapstick way,

Abbott and Costello suggested the wild, illogical comedy of the silent days. (Their trek down memory lane also included filmed "meetings" with Dr. Jekyll and Mr. Hyde, Frankenstein, the Invisible Man, and the Mummy.)

In 1957, Robert Youngson, a writer-producer-director of some note (his short subjects had won him two Oscars and two more nominations), put together a string of clips from old comedies under the title *The Golden Age of Comedy*. Among the vintage stars represented were Laurel and Hardy, Will Rogers, Ben Turpin, Harry Langdon, Billy Bevan, Mabel Normand, Carole Lombard, and Jean Harlow. Some observers criticized the absence of such as Charlie Chaplin and W.C. Fields, but this was a bit unrealistic. Anyone in Youngson's position had to content himself with what was available to him, and while no one of these compilation films could reasonably be regarded as definitive,

Abbott and Costello Meet the Keystone Kops. **The comedy team sought to evoke the era of Sennett's great silents. (U-I, 1955)**

The Golden Age of Comedy. Mabel Normand in a precari-
ous pose from one of her silent era comedies. (DCA, 1958)

most of them served the dual purposes of acquaint-
ing new fans with the work of early cinema artists,
and also making a buck for the packager.

Chaplin, who was *persona non grata* in the
United States at the time, was unable to arrest a
thriving business on this side of the ocean in
bootlegged Chaplin films. Countless saloons featuring "Gay Nineties" or "Roaring Twenties" entertainment featured periodic silent movies on their
screens, and scratchy prints of early Chaplin films
were almost invariably included. Nor was there
anything to stop any theater operator who could
get his hands on a Chaplin movie from showing it,
for a profit, without paying Chaplin a penny.

In addition, there were in circulation several
compilations of Chaplin clips, with titles like
Charlie Chaplin Carnival, *Charlie Chaplin Cavalcade*, and *Charlie Chaplin Festival*. Whatever his
political fortunes may have been, it seems, there

The Golden Age of Comedy. That's early comedian Billy
Bevan at the wheel. (DCA, 1958)

was always some audience for Chaplin films,
especially the early shorts.

By 1959, Chaplin had been living in Europe for
a decade and the jingoist heat that had driven him
out of America had cooled somewhat. Riding the
nostalgia wave of the time, an entrepreneur named

Chase Me Charlie. The scene is from a Charlie Chaplin film called *A Night at the Show.* (Citation Films, 1959)

Edwin G. O'Brien put together a string of Chaplin's early films for Essanay and called it *Chase Me Charlie.* With him were two of his favorite supporting players of the time, Ben Turpin and Edna Purviance. Notable in this collection was *A Night in the Show* (1916), in which Chaplin played two roles: Mr. Pest, a gentleman in evening clothes at a concert, and Mr. Rowdy, a bum in the balcony.

By 1960, the nostalgia binge was going full force, still focussed on early comics, and Robert Youngson again came up with a compilation of silents, this one more successful than *The Golden Age of Comedy.* The "new" film was titled *When Comedy Was King,* and employed the celluloid services of Charlie Chaplin, Buster Keaton, Laurel and Hardy, Harry Langdon, Ben Turpin, Fatty Arbuckle, Gloria Swanson, Mabel Normand, Wallace Beery, Chester Conklin, the Keystone Cops, and more.

The movie was a big success and led to yet another Robert Youngson exercise in compilation

When Comedy Was King. Among the many early comedians included in this compilation were Laurel and Hardy. (20th Century-Fox, 1960)

167

Days of Thrills and Laughter. Pearl White, in one of her cliff-hanging serials, pulls a gun on the chauffeur. (20th Century-Fox, 1961)

in 1961, entitled *Days of Thrills and Laughter.* Many of the same famous comedians turned up again, as well as Douglas Fairbanks, Harry Houdini, Boris Karloff, Warner Oland, and the inimitable Pearl White. The emphasis this time was as much on thrills and spills and narrow escapes as on hilarious sight gags of the Sennett era.

In 1962, the recycling fad attracted the attention of Harold Lloyd, some of whose old gold was assembled into *Harold Lloyd's World of Comedy.* Lloyd himself supervised the compilation, which included scenes from *Safety Last, The Freshman, Feet First, Girl Shy, Why Worry?,* and *Movie Crazy.* Lloyd, who had been off the screen since the mid-1930s (with the exception of *Mad Wednesday,* in 1951, which flopped), was a revelation to younger film goers and a remembered joy to older ones. (A second compilation, *Harold Lloyd's Funny Side of Life,* was issued in 1966, its chief distinction being a new on-camera introduction by Lloyd.)

Days of Thrills and Laughter. The famous Keystone Cops in a typical maneuver. (20th Century-Fox, 1961)

The Walter Reade-Sterling Group got into the recycling business in 1961 with *The Great Chase,* which had film clips involving such as Buster Keaton, Lillian Gish, and Douglas Fairbanks, Jr. Miss Gish was represented by *Way Down East,* Keaton by *The General,* and there was even a scene from a 1912 D.W. Griffith film, *A Girl and Her Trust.* But the film did not prove as successful as the Youngson compilations.

That resourceful man came up with still more old movies to delight new audiences. In 1963, he put together *30 Years of Fun,* again with Chaplin, Keaton, Laurel and Hardy, and more of the old favorites. But this time, in his efforts to adapt to contemporary theater requirements, Youngson expanded his old clips to large screen size, and the different dimensions resulted in snipping off some heads and feet, losing some priceless bits of comic

business, and arousing the ire of a few film critics. Nevertheless, there was much to be admired in this Youngson collection, including Chaplin's *The Rink,* one of the great comedian's most engaging films, made in 1916.

And still Youngson had not run out of films to clip, proven gold to be recycled. In 1964, he wrote and produced MGM's *Big Parade of Comedy,* this time relying on more recent films and restricted, of course, to material available at that studio. This, however, was no great hindrance, since MGM by this time had a huge backlog of cinematic gold in its vaults. The stars included John Gilbert, Marion Davies, Clark Gable, Myrna Loy, Greta Garbo, Laurel and Hardy, Cary Grant, Katharine Hepburn, W.C. Fields, Bert Lahr, the Marx Brothers, and several more.

Some critics, not yet nostalgic for anything with

Harold Lloyd's World of Comedy. **This scene from the compilation was from** *The Freshman.* **(Continental Distributing, 1962)**

169

The Great Chase. This exercise in recycling included a clip
from the D.W. Griffith 1912 film, *A Girl and Her Trust.*
The girl is Dorothy Bernard. (Reade-Sterling, 1963)

30 Years of Fun. This was still another compilation put
together by Robert Youngson, showing highlights of early
movie comedy. (20th Century-Fox, 1963)

MGM's Big Parade of Comedy. This collection included
Bert Lahr and Lucille Ball in a 1944 musical, *Meet the
People.* (MGM, 1964)

a sound track, found this compilation a cut below Youngson's other efforts, but that did not bother audiences who were happy to look at early Garbo or William Powell or Lupe Velez. And although it was not realized then, MGM's *Big Parade of Comedy* was just the tip of an enormous iceberg that was to come into full view a decade later.

Meanwhile, Youngson came back again in 1965 with a more acceptable item — *Laurel and Hardy's Laughing 20s.* Television had long since unearthed a big audience for the inspired antics of those two comedians, and it was inevitable that sooner or later someone would think of stringing together bits from some of their funnier films for theater release. By now, Youngson was the acknowledged past master of recycling, and the compilation delighted Laurel and Hardy fans, young and old.

Also in 1965, another veteran Hollywood collector turned up to claim his slice of the nostalgia pie. That was Ken Murray, who had started taking "home movies" of the stars in their relatively unguarded moments years before, notably in the "Screen Snapshots" series.

Ken Murray's Hollywood, as his 1965 compilation was titled, was something special. Besides the 110-minute film, featuring highlights of almost four decades of Murray's informal filming, the cigar-chomping comedian himself appeared on stage, providing a running commentary on the soundless film footage. Virtually every big star in the history of Hollywood was captured, at one time or another, by Murray's roving camera, and this compilation was unique in that it consisted not of theater films remembered by veteran movie buffs but of candid, informal shots of the stars at play, at work, or strolling around the famous sights of Hollywood and its environs.

The compilation/recycling fever spread, of course, to other, less inventive entrepreneurs. In 1965, the Walter Reade-Sterling Group came up with *The Love Goddesses,* which meant random shots of Theda Bara, Mae West, Marlene Dietrich, Jean Harlow, Brigitte Bardot, Elizabeth Taylor, Lana Turner, and, naturally, Marilyn Monroe. Although it was an interesting idea (since aped by several television specials) the film did not have too great an impact on the box office.

Even though the younger television audience had long since "discovered" W.C. Fields, it was not until 1966 that a compilation of that great clown's

films was issued, under the title *W.C. Fields Comedy Festival.*

But it was worth waiting for. Included were scenes from such Fields features as *The Bank Dick* and *Never Give a Sucker an Even Break,* and earlier shorts like *The Fatal Glass of Beer,* and *The Dentist.*

The inexhaustible Robert Youngson put together *The Further Perils of Laurel and Hardy* (1968), which had clips from *Flying Elephants, Sugar Daddies, Do Detectives Think?,* and others originally done for Hal Roach. As a bonus, there were glimpses of Jean Harlow, Charlie Chase, and other L and H associates of those early days.

And in 1970, Youngson again scored with a package of recycled gold entitled *Four Clowns.* The four were Laurel and Hardy, Buster Keaton, and Charlie Chase. Keaton was shown in *Seven Chances,* a gem; and Chase, too often overlooked, was seen in *Limousine Love,* one of his best short subjects.

By now, the nostalgia wave had become a torrent, outreaching by far the limits of early cinema comedians. Audiences were buying freshly minted nostalgia — new antiques, as it were. Films like *The Last Picture Show, Paper Moon,* and *What's Up, Doc?* had established Peter Bogdanovich as the new (and young) leader of an old wave. Bogdanovich seemed determined to prove that he could do again what Howard Hawks, Gregory La Cava, and other 1930s directors had done so successfully. And audiences were lapping it up.

And while new movies of old times were turning up everywhere — *The Great Gatsby, The Sting, Chinatown, American Grafitti, Sounder, Dillinger* — there was still enough nostalgia going around to accommodate yet one more compilation film, this one something of a landmark in looking back.

This time, however, it was not the busy Mr. Youngson who did the patch-up job, but Jack Haley, Jr., son of the veteran movie comedian and a seasoned television producer in his own right. The film was MGM's mammoth *That's Entertainment,* and it appealed to the public so much that on its first round of play dates it took in a phenomenal $40,000,000.

It was clearly a superior entertainment, skillfully put together, calculated to nudge a nostalgic tear from the most skeptical eye by its effective juxtaposing of then-and-now. We saw not only the

The Love Goddesses. Among the sex queens glimpsed were Brigitte Bardot in *Love is My Profession.* At left, Jean Gabin. (Continental Distributing, 1965).

W.C. Fields Comedy Festival. This clip was from *Never Give a Sucker an Even Break.* With Fields is Leon Errol. (Realart, 1966)

The Further Perils of Laurel and Hardy. That's Stan in drag and Ollie looking worried. (20th Century-Fox, 1968)

4 Clowns. The one above is Charlie Chase, caught in the act of holding up a movie theater. (20th Century-Fox, 1970)

That's Entertainment. Fred Astaire and Gene Kelly revisit what's left of a big MGM set for *The Bandwagon.* (MGM, 1974)

That's Entertainment, Part 2. **More of the same, once more with Astaire and Kelly threading together the excerpts from earlier Metro hits. (MGM, 1976)**

young Astaire and Kelly dancing as if there were no law of gravity, but the older Astaire and Kelly talking about the good old days at Metro. We were treated to part of a musical number from *The Band Wagon,* filmed in a train station set; and we also saw what is left of that MGM set today, dust-covered, peeling paint, cobwebs and all.

The hosting chores also engaged Bing Crosby, Donald O'Connor, James Stewart, Liza Minelli, and Frank Sinatra, and their very puffiness and paunchiness (excepting Liza, of course) somehow added poignancy to the whole sentimental exercise.

Predictably, there was soon talk of Warner Brothers making their own nostalgic compilation of excerpts from past musicals (*Dames, 42nd Street,* the Gold Diggers films would certainly yield some good footage) to be titled *Hooray for Hollywood.* For some reason, however, that one never did get off the ground. A film so titled was

made in 1976 (produced by Edward S. Shaw and distributed by a company called Cinamco) but attracted little attention. Yet another attempt to cash in on the success of *That's Entertainment* was *Meanwhile, Back at the Ranch.* This compilation featured such old Western stars as Tom Mix, Buck Jones, and Roy Rogers, but it, too, went largely unnoticed. Similarly, compilations of excerpts from old 20th Century-Fox and Columbia films were strung together in ninety-minute "salutes" to those studios, but these were shown on late-night television rather than being released as theater features.

Just as MGM had been preeminent in creating the most lavish of movie musicals, that studio seemed again to lead the pack in recycling its old gold. The singular success of *That's Entertainment* led, inevitably, to a sequel called *That's Entertainment, Part II,* released in 1976.

Although this one wasn't quite the box-office bonanza its predecessor had been, it was nevertheless a respectable success and some critics preferred it to the earlier film. This time, Fred Astaire and Gene Kelly took care of all the hosting chores and even did a few dance routines together (at ages seventy-seven and sixty-four, respectively) and the film also included samples of Laurel and Hardy, Abbott and Costello, and the Marx Brothers. Also featured were such Metro stalwarts as Judy Garland, Mickey Rooney, Freddie Bartholomew, and Kathryn Grayson.

The movie studios might be auctioning off their old costumes and props, turning over their back lots and ranches to oil drillers and land developers. But they still had some gold in their film vaults, and it seemed likely that what MGM did with their old musicals might as well be done by other studios with dramas, comedies, or "tributes" to particular stars.

Any industry in which one studio can rake in forty million bucks on just one chunk of recycled material can hardly be considered washed up.

9 Hollywood Digs Deeper

Before attempting to bring this survey more or less up to date, let us consider for a moment the use of the word Hollywood in a generic rather than a geographical sense.

A good many other countries in the world have long since developed their own cinema art and/or industries. There are many, both in America and elsewhere, who consider that the films of Italy, France, Britain, Sweden and elsewhere are, by and large, superior to those from America. Certainly it would be reckless to dismiss the achievements of Bergman, Fellini, Godard, Antonioni, Kurosawa, Lean, Truffaut, and other internationally renowned filmmakers.

But this is a book about Hollywood, and particularly Hollywood's treatment of Hollywood subjects and people. Still, it is worth noting that, now and then, filmmakers in other countries have used filmmaking as thematic material. More important, perhaps, in some cases they have emulated Hollywood attitudes in doing so. Or, put another way, perhaps movie people in Rome, Paris, or London are as large a target as they are in Hollywood and must, in the view of filmmakers there, be presented as glamorous, phoney, vain, grasping, or just plain foolish. In any case, that seems to have happened in some of the foreign-made films dealing with movie people.

One example was Fellini's 1963 film, *8½* (so titled because it was his seventh feature film, and he had also made three shorts). His protagonist, played by Marcello Mastroianni, was a jaded film director, spoiled rotten from childhood on, who feels trapped and stifled as he is about to embark on a new film venture. Parading through his life are wives, mistresses, dream girls, sycophants, models, writers — all the stock characters one might find in a Hollywood film about Hollywood. Being the perceptive director he is, Fellini managed to present these people with rather more honesty than one would find in the average Hollywood exercise of similar scope. But one is left to wonder if all the excesses, self-indulgence, and greed one has come to associate with Hollywood are not just as prevalent in other film centers throughout the world. (Earlier, in 1961, *La Dolce Vita,* Fellini's abrasive comment on the corruption of contemporary Roman society, included a glimpse of a pathetically ludicrous Hollywood sex goddess, played by Anita Ekberg.)

John Schlesinger's 1965 film, *Darling,* had a hint of Fellini's *La Dolce Vita,* transferred to London, but also recalled *The Barefoot Contessa* as it recounted the bizarre career of a flighty, selfish young lady (Julie Christie) in her quest of fame and fortune, starting as a model and ending up — in

Darling. Julie Christie's dizzy career was sardonically observed by Dirk Bogarde. (Embassy, 1965)

that peculiarly logical chain of events that contemporary life seems to have made inevitable — a lonely celebrity.

A more conventional imitation of Hollywood was *Swinger's Paradise* (1965), another English production directed by Sidney J. Furie. This one utilized the name and talents of Cliff Richard, then a top pop star in Britain, in a story right out of Hollywood, circa 1938. It involved a group of youngsters on a cruise ship who land on a desert island and decide to film their experiences. (How many times did Mickey Rooney or Judy Garland or Donald O'Connor say: "Hey, gang, I've got a great idea. We can put on the show right here in this barn."?) Conveniently on hand is Walter Slezak as a moviemaker, and he and the kids pool their resources to turn out a smash hit. It was, to be charitable, neither Furie's nor Britain's finest hour and a half.

The year before, the justifiably esteemed Jean-

Swinger's Paradise. The glum look on the faces of Walter Slezak and Cliff Richard were no less than the film deserved. (American-International, 1965)

Contempt. Film producer Jack Palance had eyes for Brigitte Bardot, the wife of his hired writer. (Embassy, 1964)

Luc Godard came close to falling on his face by trying to walk the slender wire of satire, ignoring, as have so many others, the shrewd definition of some legendary hard-headed producer: "Satire is what closes on Saturday night."

The Godard film was *Contempt,* with Jack Palance, Brigitte Bardot, Michel Piccoli, and, playing himself, veteran director Fritz Lang. Palance was a pretentious film producer who hired writer Piccoli to do a script for him; Bardot was Piccoli's ambivalent wife who was puzzled that her husband should allow Palance to make passes at her and finally caught one of them; and Piccoli was the stereotypical writer, torn between the itch for success and the wish for integrity. Unhappily, Godard's attempt to satirize movie-types fell into the familiar trap of merely imitating the thing being satirized.

Francois Truffaut directed perhaps the best foreign-made film about movie people. This was *Day for Night* (1973) and it displayed Truffaut's keen understanding of the heartbreak as well as the idiocy of filmmaking.

Truffaut appeared as a film director, steering the hectic production of a movie that all concerned come to realize is not worth the effort. He is surrounded by an unstable leading lady (Jacqueline Bisset), a wreck of a movie lover (Jean-Pierre Aumont), a besotted character actress (Valentina Cortesa), a materialistic producer (Jean Champion) and other familiar "Hollywood" types. It is to Truffaut's credit that he managed to present these characters as both hilarious and rather pathetic, and his film says more about the tribulations of moviemaking than most of the films on the subject, of whatever origin.

Meanwhile, back on the home front, movies about Hollywood — or its far-flung representatives — continued to turn up with increasing regularity, if erratic results.

There was, as could be expected, more shlock on the market than ever before. There are those who are content to regard *Myra Breckinridge* (1970) as the absolute nadir of filmmaking, but all the returns are not in yet.

The movie based on Gore Vidal's sexational novel was, by any yardstick, unperfumed garbage. One would think that any picture that turns Rex Reed into Raquel Welch cannot be all bad, but that's not taking into account the scenery-chewing of John Huston, the embarrassing comeback of Mae West, looking like a swollen prune, and the almost total abandonment of anything resembling wit in exchange for sophomoric bad taste. The story was, if you will forgive the expression, laid in Hollywood.

The same year brought us another coil of proof that raw film might better be cut up for mandolin picks than exposed before inept actors in a worthless script. This was *Beyond the Valley of the Dolls* (1970), to which even Jacqueline Susann, author of the parent story, objected. Like its predecessor, it dealt with some of the more kinky aspects of show business life, updated to the extent that the characters are rock musicians and groupies instead of ambitious models and agents. Russ Meyer, hitherto a maker of medium-core pornography, turned his grasp of the seedy side of life to this procession of lesbians, hermaphrodites, top-heavy predators, unmacho males, and other unfortunates. If *Valley of the Dolls* was racy soap opera, this "sequel" was sticky grime opera.

Miss Susann is gone (she died in 1974) but not yet forgotten. Her next published novel, *Once is Not Enough,* was filmed in 1975, proving only that Hollywood still cannot resist a best-seller, whatever its merits. This time, Miss Susann's cast of char-

Day For Night. Francois Truffaut, facing front, directed and also played a director in this study of the woes of moviemaking. (Warner Brothers, 1973)

Myra Breckinridge. Raquel Welch and John Huston were among the culprits in this temple of tastelessness. (20th Century-Fox, 1970)

Beyond the Valley of the Dolls. Edy Williams and David Gurian in one of the quieter moments of this mindless marathon of soft-core pornography. (20th Century-Fox, 1970)

acters included a has-been movie producer (Kirk Douglas again) so broke that he marries a wealthy woman (Alexis Smith) who just wants a husband to cover up her long-running lesbian romance with an ex-movie star (Melina Mercouri) of similar proclivities.

Films like this one and *Myra Breckinridge* and *Beyond the Valley of the Dolls* were really a throw-back to the old Hollywood exposé movies, somewhat aided by today's more permissive atmosphere. They were just digging up fictionalized dirt, but the new rules allowed them to dig deeper.

The early 1970s also saw another rash of mock horror movies involving Hollywood. One of these was *The House that Dripped Blood* (1971), an omnibus film that included a story called *The Cloak,* in which Jon Pertwee as an egotistical horror movie star demanded authentic costumes and wound up wearing an honest-to-goodness vampire's cloak, which obviously made him thirsty for human blood.

Then there was *Madhouse* (1974), in which Vincent Price, an old hand at mock horror, played a horror film star embarking on a comeback trail, only to be betrayed by another veteran horror-film type, Peter Cushing. The film also had cameo appearances by Basil Rathbone and Boris Karloff, part of the old horror movie gang.

Also in 1974, there was *The Phantom of Hollywood,* originally made for television but later released to theaters, which had a mysterious phantom terrorizing a movie studio. The cast included Jack Cassidy, Broderick Crawford, John Ireland, Peter Lawford, and Skye Aubrey.

Perhaps the most important of this ring of horror films dealing with movie types was *Targets* (1968), partly because it launched the career of Peter Bogdanovich. Besides appearing in his own first feature (as a young director) Bogdanovich had the services of Boris Karloff, as a veteran horror film star now intrigued by the subject of mindless sniper killings. Whatever its shortcomings, the movie put Bogdanovich on the cinema map and also indicated there was renewed interest in Karloff. By the middle of the 1970s, Hollywood was plunging into a whole sea of new film biographies of hitherto unexamined stars of the past.

In the meantime, nonbiographical movies about Hollywood people — good, bad, or indifferent — continued to turn up. In 1968, Kim Novak struck out again in *The Legend of Lylah Clare,* playing a starlet cast to play in a film biography of a fictitious star named Lylah Clare. As usually happens in these stories, she gradually begins to take on the traits of the doomed woman she is playing, and you can see the tragic ending coming about half way through the film. The cast included Peter Finch, Ernest Borgnine, and Milton Seltzer, but the biggest problem was that Kim Novak was no more Lylah Clare than she had been Jeanne Eagels or, for that matter, Moll Flanders.

Bob & Carol & Ted & Alice (1969) was a superficially amusing comedy about the new morality that reflected more the ambiance of Southern California than of Hollywood. Bob, played by Robert Culp, was a documentary filmmaker, but that was almost incidental. But the film is worth including here for two reasons: first, because the manners and mores of the Hollywood set had by now spread beyond the professional boundaries of people in the film business to include people who lived in the same part of the world; and second, because the film reflected a Hollywood truism, namely that the packaging might scream modernity, but inside it was still old-fashioned romantic. For all the talk about sexual liberation, the two couples backed away from the planned mini-orgy, no doubt because the filmmakers felt that was still what audiences wanted them to do.

Marlo Thomas, hitherto a successful television star, switched to the big screen for *Jenny* (1970), a nicely sentimental story with contemporary trim-

Once is Not Enough. Melina Mercouri and Alexis Smith share a tender moment during the absence of Miss Smith's current husband. (Paramount, 1975)

The House that Dripped Blood. An orthodontist might have helped Ingrid Pitt, but the script's trouble was terminal. (Cinerama, 1971)

Madhouse. Vincent Price, slightly charred, was mad at the movie world in this mock horror film. (American-International, 1974)

The Phantom of Hollywood. Skye Aubrey, as the daughter of a movie tycoon, is kidnapped by a transient phantom. (MGM, 1974)

Targets. Peter Bogdanovich both directed and appeared in this, his first, film, along with Boris Karloff. (Paramount, 1969)

The Legend of Lylah Clare. Kim Novak wastes good wine by pouring it over Peter Finch. But the film used was a greater waste. (MGM, 1968)

Bob & Carol & Ted & Alice. Robert Culp and Elliott Gould, sans wives, talk over their marital problems. (Columbia, 1969)

Jenny. **Alan Alda and Marlo Thomas co-starred in this love story of a couple of movie buffs. (ABC Pictures, 1970)**

mings. She is an unmarried pregnant girl who marries a filmmaker (Alan Alda) and then falls in love with him. He marries her to avoid the draft, and eventually falls for her. There were some touches of gentle humor — both being film buffs, they consider naming the baby Jean-Luc, in honor of Godard — and some good performances by the supporting cast (notably Vincent Gardenia and Marian Hailey), but the movie, like *Bob & Carol, et al,* was far more conventional than it pretended to be.

Cover Me, Babe (1970) tried earnestly to show us the dilemma of a contemporary student filmmaker, determined to escape the corrupting influences of Hollywood and do his own thing. The biggest trouble with the film was that, judging by the evidence, the young filmmaker's own thing was a bloody bore. Robert Forster played the role, Sandra Locke was the girl who believed in him, and Ken Kercheval and Susanne Benton were among the other student filmmakers who considered Forster something of a budding genius.

Surely more conventional but vastly more entertaining was one of the characters played by Walter Matthau in Neil Simon's transplanted stage hit, *Plaza Suite* (1971). Matthau played an aging Hollywood producer who returns to New York's Plaza Hotel and attempts to seduce Barbara Harris, his onetime girl friend from New Jersey. This was easily the most amusing of the three stories that made up the film.

Paul Mazursky and Larry Tucker, who scored a big commercial hit with *Bob & Carol & Ted & Alice,* were faced with the problem of how to top it. So they decided on a movie about a film director who had scored a big commercial hit and was then faced with the problem of how to top it. It was called *Alex in Wonderland* (1970) and had Donald Sutherland as the director, Ellen Burstyn as his wife, and cameo appearances by Federico Fellini and Jeanne Moreau. In the view of some critics, Mazursky and Tucker failed in their groping

Plaza Suite. Walter Matthau was a rumpled roué from Hollywood in one of Neil Simon's three stories that made up this film. (Paramount, 1971)

Alex in Wonderland. Donald Sutherland, left, played a director trying to decide what to direct. (MGM, 1970)

Cover Me, Babe. Ken Kercheval and Susanne Benton were student actors in this story of "modern" filmmakers. (20th Century-Fox, 1970)

The Last Movie. Dennis Hopper both directed and starred
in this strange study of a movie crew on location in Peru.
(Universal, 1971)

search for a subject as much as did the character they created for *Alex in Wonderland*.

Dennis Hopper, another new filmmaker whose *Easy Rider* had achieved astonishing success, turned inward to examine filmmaking in his 1971 effort, *The Last Movie*. (Some audiences may have got this mixed up with Bogdanovich's *The Last Picture Show*, a far superior film that had nothing to do with moviemaking.) Hopper tried to show the effects of a visiting Hollywood movie company on the Indian inhabitants of a small village in Peru. The film being made was about Billy the Kid, and the actor playing him (Hopper) hangs around the village after the end of filming while the Indians pretend to make a movie based on the Passion Play, with Hopper as Jesus. Whatever Hopper's murky symbolism was intended to prove, all *The Last Movie* proved was that Hopper was as unsure of what his next project should be as Mazursky and Tucker had been.

Still it is interesting to note that the beginning of the 1970s brought a renewed interest by filmmakers in depicting the agonies and the ecstasies of filmmaking. Sometimes this resulted in some dull contemplation of navels, other times it brought us some good entertainment.

Not to be taken too seriously was *The Phynx* (1970), which involved a Monkees-like rock group, formed specifically to function as secret agents. Their mission was to rescue some show biz types from Iron Curtain captivity. But what saved the film was the sprinkling of nostalgia it offered, for among those to be glimpsed in cameo roles were Edgar Bergen and Charlie McCarthy, Ed Sullivan, Patti Andrews, Johnny Weissmuller, Maureen O'Sullivan, Dick Clark, Joan Blondell, Xavier Cugat, and Joe Louis.

The best line was delivered by another movie veteran, Pat O'Brien, who observed woefully that if he'd played "the other part" in some of those old Warner Brothers films he'd be in Sacramento "and Ronald Reagan would be here."

In 1971, chunky Chuck McCann was starred in *The Projectionist*, a sort of combination of Superman and Walter Mitty. McCann was the projectionist in a New York theater who day-dreamed during his spare moments, becoming Captain Flash and rescuing the girl of his dreams from all manner of peril. Naturally, the theater manager — his boss, played by comedian Rodney Dangerfield — was The Bat in McCann's fantasies. Despite its failings,

The Phynx. Johnny Weissmuller and Maureen O'Sullivan, once Tarzan and Jane, were among the veterans in this bit of camp nostalgia. (Warner Brothers, 1970)

The Projectionist. Chuck McCann and Ina Balin in one of the scenes imagined by projectionist McCann. (Maron Films, 1971)

The Projectionist had the merit of indicating how easily an imaginative movie buff can project himself into the fantasies on the screen.

Another amusing look at movie types was *Pulp* (1972), made in Europe but decidedly American in outlook. It was about a faded movie tough guy (Mickey Rooney) now living in a Mediterranean villa, who hires a writer (Michael Caine) to pen his memoirs. Somewhat reminiscent of George Raft, the Rooney character has had some shady associations in the past, and his old cronies now decide to bump him off before he can tell his story to the would-be Mickey Spillane played by Caine. Above all else, Rooney's portrait of a washed-up Hollywood tough guy was hilarious.

More serious, at least in its intention, was *Play It As It Lays* (1972), based on Joan Didion's successful novel about the disintegration of a Hollywood girl whose life has gone awry. Tuesday Weld was impressive in the leading role, trying to summon pleasant memories as if she were looking for solid chunks of meat in a watery soup. Anthony Perkins was good, too, as the girl's only friend, a disillusioned Hollywood type on the verge of suicide. But the film tried so hard to be authentically "in" that it tended to leave audiences confused, if vaguely moved.

That same year, Paul Morrissey directed and Andy Warhol produced *Heat,* a kind of melancholy spoof of *Sunset Boulevard.* Joe Dallesandro was a washed-up former child actor, hanging around a seedy Hollywood motel, surrounded by some typically Warholian bizarre characters. Perhaps the most appealing — and surely the most professional — was Sylvia Miles, as an aging actress. At the end of *Heat,* Miss Miles attempts to shoot Dallesandro (as Swanson had done to Holden in the famous Billy Wilder film). But the gun doesn't go off and she flings it into the pool.

Hollywood exposé was far more slickly portrayed in *The Last of Sheila* (1973), directed by Herbert Ross from an original screenplay by Stephen Sondheim and Anthony Perkins. The fine cast included James Coburn, Richard Benjamin, James Mason, Dyan Cannon, Raquel Welch, Joan Hackett, and Ian McShane.

Coburn played an eccentric film producer whose wife (Sheila) was killed by a hit-and-run driver. A year later, he invites six "friends" on a Mediterranean cruise aboard his yacht — also named Sheila. The six, it developes, all are possible

Pulp. Hood Lionel Stander and ghost writer Michael Caine in a scene from this comedy about a washed-up Hollywood tough guy. (United Artists, 1972)

Play It as it Lays. Hollywood decadence is represented here by Ruth Ford, drinks, cards, and a beach boy. (Universal, 1972)

Heat. Joe Dallesandro and Sylvia Miles were both washed-up Hollywood types in this Andy Warhol-Paul Morrissey effort. (Levitt-Pickman Film Corp., 1972)

The Last of Sheila. James Coburn, at head of table, lured some friends into a hair-raising game to reveal the killer of his wife. (Warner Brothers, 1973)

suspects in the hit-and-run accident, and Coburn devises a game intended to unveil the killer. He knows their secrets (one is a kleptomaniac, one an ex-convict, one a homosexual, etc.) and drops clues that will force his guests to confess them. Eventually, Coburn is himself killed and the film narrows down to a cat-and-mouse game between Mason and Benjamin, with the audience trying to guess which of them is the killer.

Although *The Last of Sheila* had little to do with filmmaking, its characters were all mid-1970s Hollywood types, their talk brittle, hip, sometimes coarse; their values and references all connected to movie work. They may not seem admirable, but they certainly seem interesting. The film was really an old-fashioned murder mystery, but the style and the characters were contemporary.

Somewhat akin to *The Projectionist,* and rather funnier, was *Play It Again, Sam* (1972), which

Play it Again, Sam. Woody Allen, in a romantic moment with Diane Keaton, has to summon up the image of Bogie to know how to handle it. (Paramount, 1972)

189

Woody Allen first wrote for the stage and then translated to the screen, with himself as the star. As the title implied, Allen played a man so insecure, so near total collapse, that only the summoned-up image of a screen idol like Humphrey Bogart can give him the courage to get through his life.

Not quite as zany as some of Allen's films, this one had rather more cohesion, without entirely inhibiting Allen's penchant for irreverent and irrelevant one-liners. In his irresistably mad way, Allen was telling us that a lot of us still live in the dream world of the movies — and that maybe it's just as well.

Although made in Canada and based on a witty book by Canadian author Mordecai Richler, *The Apprenticeship of Duddy Kravitz* (1974) deserves inclusion here because it gave us one of the most incisive satires on a pretentious moviemaker ever committed to film.

The role was played by Denholm Elliott, that fine English actor whose talent far exceeds his fame. Elliott was one of those washed-up film-makers cadging drinks in Montreal, condescending to take on so prosaic an assignment as filming a bar mitzvah for huckster Kravitz (Richard Dreyfuss), and then helplessly driven to turn it into such a piece of arty trash that the uncultured backer who ordered it is too stunned to realize he's been taken.

In various ways, the films of the early 1970s were giving us some arresting portraits of movie people, some more funny than in the old days of kidding Hollywood lightly. Denholm Elliott, in *The Apprenticeship of Duddy Kravitz,* was pathetically funny partly because writer Richler had such a strong (and unflattering) opinion of filmmakers. However murkily drawn, *Play It As It Lays* evoked sadness because Tuesday Weld conveyed the emptiness of a seemingly glamorous career gone astray.

In *The Exorcist* (1973), that shockingly successful modern Gothic, Ellen Burstyn was a film actress on location when the devil came to call. But she was a film actress of the 1970s, spitting out saltier language on screen than Carole Lombard probably did in private four decades earlier.

Shampoo (1975) was, in a way, the most important of these films, although its connection with movie people was tenuous. It presented a vivid dissection of the world around Hollywood — Beverly Hills, Bel Air, investment counsellors, neglected wives, television commercial directors,

The Apprenticeship of Duddy Kravitz. Richard Dreyfuss, right, was Duddy. At left is Denholm Elliott, who played a boozy film director hard pressed for money. (Paramount, 1974)

starlets, mistresses, and a stud of a hairdresser who made Alfie look like Little Lord Fauntleroy. This last role was expertly played by Warren Beatty, who also produced the movie and co-wrote it with Robert Towne.

Superficially, *Shampoo* was like a French farce, with philandering husbands and wives all but tripping over each other's illicit and frenzied couplings. But underneath that was a mirror of Southern California society, circa 1968, on the very night Richard Nixon and Spiro Agnew were first elevated to the country's top public offices. It was an ugly mirror image, with cynicism, selfishness, loveless love-making, moral and ethical bankruptcy all revealed against a counterpoint of pious hope (expressed in television speeches by Nixon and Agnew) of restoring America to a higher moral course.

If it did not deal explicitly with movie people, *Shampoo* nevertheless gave us a look at a life style surely influenced by the pace set by the Hollywood colony. It might reasonably be argued that people like these might as easily exist in Atlanta or Dallas or New York, but it cannot be denied that these particular people seemed most natural in Beverly Hills, Bel Air, and the Los Angeles canyons; and if they weren't movie people, they had certainly learned to ape what they regarded as the chic mores of authentic Hollywood fauna.

Shampoo was interesting, too, in that it reflected yet another pattern of the movies of the mid-1970s. It intentionally set its action back a

The Exorcist. Jason Miller and Ellen Burstyn. She played a film actress on location in Washington when the devil took control of her daughter. (Warner Brothers, 1973)

specific number of years (to 1968) to point up its view, whatever one may think of it, that the election of Nixon and the signs of disintegration of the moral fabric of America were not merely coincidental.

This represented a different approach to nostalgia, but it still utilized nostalgia. In a different way, so did *The Way We Were* (1973), with Barbra Streisand and Robert Redford. This comedy-drama went back to the late 1930s, then came up to the 1950s, tracing the bumpy romance of a college radical (Streisand) and her upper-crust Wasp man (Redford) up to the point of his success in Hollywood as a writer. But while it touched on the ugly stain of the McCarthy-era witch hunts, *The Way We Were* never really came to grips with it, thus remaining more a nostalgic romance rather than a vital social commentary.

The real wave of nostalgia hit its stride in 1975, when John Schlesinger's version of the highly regarded Nathaniel West story, *The Day of the Locust*, reached the screen.

West's gloomy vision of Hollywood (written in the 1930s) as the gathering place of born losers, the site of the apocalypse, stressed the author's dismay at the world around him. Schlesinger meticulously reproduced the texture of the Hollywood of that time, but in his zeal to make a Statement rather than merely a film, he carried West's grotesque vision to such excesses of graphic horror that he somehow succeeded only in shocking audiences rather than moving them. The opening night riot that climaxed the film as well as the book is an example: what was, in the book, the protagonist's nightmare vision of what seemed to him inevitable is, in the film, so graphically spelled out that it defies credibility.

Still, Schlesinger faithfully gave us the full roster of misfit characters that peopled the novel: the young art director (William Atherton) trying to make it in films; the old vaudeville ham (Burgess

Shampoo. Warren Beatty, the Beverly Hills stud, and Julie Christie, one of his countless conquests. (Columbia, 1975)

The Way We Were. Robert Redford and Barbra Streisand took a backward look at life from the late 1930s to the McCarthy era. (Columbia, 1973)

The Day of the Locust. Robert Atherton and Donald Sutherland were among the Hollywood losers in this filming of Nathaniel West's famous story. (Paramount, 1975)

Meredith) and his movie-struck daughter (Karen Black); the wealthy Midwesterner (Donald Sutherland) who just wants to be in Hollywood; the flamboyant faith healer (Geraldine Page) theatrically urging all to repent; and a large and generally effective cast of supporting losers.

Altogether different, but again underscoring the still healthy market for nostalgia, was *The Great Waldo Pepper* (1975), with Robert Redford in the title role. Going all the way back to the First World War, it gave us a hero whose love of flying ruled his life. The tragedy of Waldo's young life was that he never got a chance to do battle with the great German ace, Ernst Kessler.

But Hollywood changes all that. Waldo eventually drifts to the movie world, to make a living stunt flying in a war movie. And who should turn up as one of the other stunt fliers but his great nemesis, Ernst Kessler, thus providing Waldo with the fulfillment of his life's dream — and the movie with a rousing finish.

The growing nostalgia market kept growing. It might be argued — and, indeed, has been — that America in the middle of the 1970s preferred to look back rather than forward, that the erosion caused by Vietnam, Watergate, energy crises, recessions, Middle East rumblings, unemployment, inflation, CIA conspiracies, and a general lack of faith in the future, made the past seem far more attractive. Perhaps there was even some comfort to be found through the realization that the past — as painted in *The Day of the Locust,* for example — was no picnic, either.

But whatever the reasons, Hollywood filmmakers were more than willing to feed the hunger for living in the past, and particularly, it seemed, for re-creating or recalling Hollywood legends.

Another 1975 example of looking back at Hollywood decadence was *The Wild Party,* with James Coco in a part reminiscent of Fatty Arbuckle, and Raquel Welch as his inexplicably loyal wife. Coco played Jolly Grimm (even the name smacked of the heavy-handed approach to the subject), a silent era comic desperately trying to make a comeback. A meaner, less likable character would be hard to imagine than Mr. Grimm, and the film offered a sordid picture of Hollywood at the end of the silent film era. The bacchanal referred to in the title (which takes up much of the movie's footage) was no more appetizing than Schlesinger's scene of carnage in *The Day of the Locust,* and *The Wild Party* was far inferior to the Schlesinger film in every way.

But Hollywood was now into a cycle of recalling its past, ignoble or otherwise, and audiences anxiously awaited each new portrait of some old star's private life.

The next to come was a kind of double feature: *Gable and Lombard,* a romantic comedy that sought to capture the glamor of two of Hollywood's most beloved superstars, as well as to follow the lead of Peter Bogdanovich in re-creating the zany comedy style of the 1930s. James Brolin, hitherto known primarily as Marcus Welby's television assistant, was cast as Gable (after Burt Reynolds turned down the part). Jill Clayburgh, a talented young actress but not too well known yet, played Lombard, the uninhibited comedienne who lassoed Gable into a happy, if brief, marriage that ended tragically with her death in an air crash while on a war bond selling tour in 1942.

Like most earlier film biographies of film

The Great Waldo Pepper. **Roderick Cook was the film director explaining to rival air aces Bo Brundin and Robert Redford the dogfight about to be filmed. (Universal, 1975)**

The Wild Party. **James Coco, as a silent screen comedian desperately trying to revitalize his career, was the central figure in this nostalgic film. (American-International, 1975)**

notables, *Gable and Lombard* took some considerable liberties with the facts, but that could have come as no surprise to anyone familiar with Hollywood tradition. Where it failed — and fail it did — was in making too much of the tribulations suffered by its principals because Gable was still married (though separated) and his studio frowned on his romance with Lombard. One critic described it as a fan magazine movie "with the emotional zap of a long-lost Louella Parsons column."

But before *Gable and Lombard* was released, the same studio (Universal) was already at work on yet another slice of Hollywood nostalgia called *W.C. Fields and Me,* a "biography" of that great and complex clown, with Rod Steiger cast as Fields and

Gable and Lombard. James Brolin was Clark Gable and Jill Clayburgh played Carole Lombard in this romantic comedy about two superstars of bygone years. (Universal, 1975)

Valerie Perrine as Carlotta Monti, Fields's longtime mistress whose memoirs formed the basis of the movie.

This time, thanks largely to an intelligent, convincing performance by Steiger, the movie was more successful, at least in giving us a glimpse of what Fields was like in his private life. Steiger concentrated less on trying to look like Fields and more on giving us some insight into the man's character — a man who was selfish, bitter, crabby, lonely, but above all unfailingly witty.

Miss Perrine was somewhat less successful as Carlotta Monti, but the film boasted two good supporting performances: by Jack Cassidy as John Barrymore, and by Billy Barty as a Fields sidekick.

Also in 1975, Warner Brothers came up with a good Raymond Chandler-type mystery that used Hollywood and the movie business as a setting. This was *Night Moves*, with Gene Hackman as a private eye hired by a former film actress to locate her missing daughter. Hackman finds the girl (Melanie Griffith) and brings her home, but he soon hears that the girl, while working as a stunt girl in a movie, has been killed.

While the story is primarily concerned with Hackman's attempts to solve a crime, the film also offers a few interesting Hollywood figures, most notably a veteran stuntman expertly played by Edward Binns.

But while *Night Moves* touched on Hollywood, it was not typical of the mid-1970s films that wallowed in film-capital nostalgia, like *W.C. Fields and Me, Gable and Lombard,* and *The Day of the Locust.*

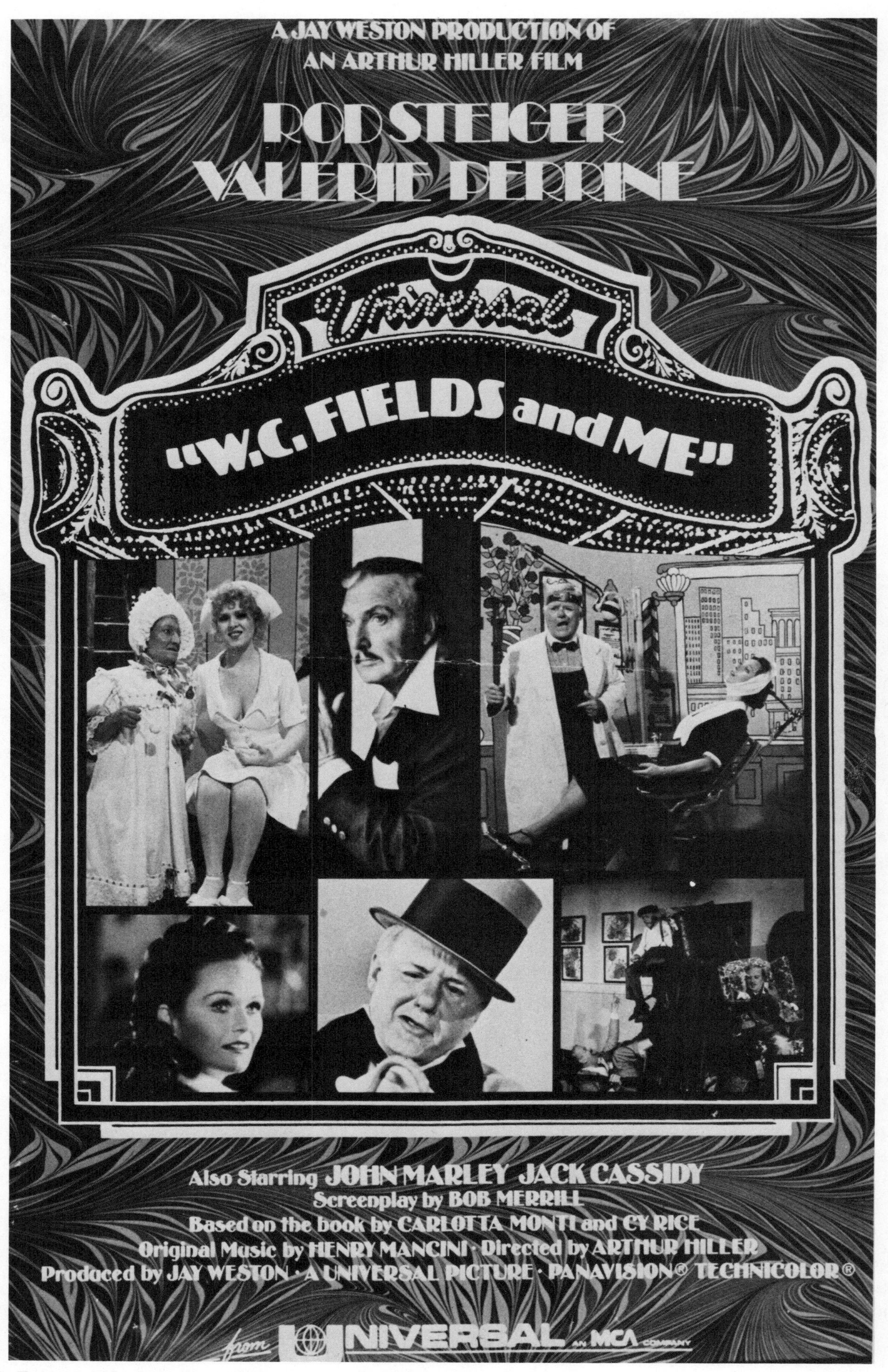

W. C. Fields and Me. Even the stylized marquee reflects the nostalgic approach to this film biography of the great comic, based on the memoirs of Carlotta Monti. Rod Steiger was seen as Fields, Valerie Perrine as Carlotta. (Universal, 1975)

Night Moves. **Gene Hackman, right, was a tough but vulnerable Hollywood private eye in this good thriller. (Warner Brothers, 1975)**

More typical, though a total disaster, was *Won Ton Ton, the Dog Who Saved Hollywood*, released by Paramount in 1976. In this one, nostalgia was totally thrown out in favor of camp. Set in the mid-twenties, the comedy involves Bruce Dern as a tour-bus driver determined to become a film producer; Art Carney as a low-budget studio head faced with bankruptcy; Madeline Kahn as an aspiring actress who is befriended by a German shepherd.

As if they realized the weaknesses of their film, the producers stuffed the cast with a small army of "cameo" players, including Ricardo Montalban, Rhonda Fleming, Dorothy Lamour, Victor Mature, Guy Madison, Zsa Zsa Gabor, Ann Miller, Milton Berle, Alice Faye, and even Henny Youngman — sixty-six of them in all, and not all of them together could do for this film what Won Ton Ton supposedly did for Hollywood.

Won Ton Ton, the Dog Who Saved Hollywood. **Art Carney and Bruce Dern were among the many skilled players who wasted their efforts in this hapless hunk of hokum based in early Hollywood. (Paramount, 1976)**

A similar fate awaited another 1976 release, *Hearts of the West,* although this film had some redeeming qualities. Nonetheless, it did so poorly at the box office that it was being shown on television by early 1977.

In truth, *Hearts of the West* deserved a better fate, if only because of its disarming ingenuousness. Jeff Bridges, its star, seemed surprisingly like the Stuart Erwin in *Make Me A Star* (nee *Merton of the Movies*). He played an Iowa farm boy of the 1930s, determined to become a writer of Western stories. Recklessly, he goes to Nevada to find the "college" he wants to attend, naively unaware that this is simply a correspondence course dodge run by a couple of seedy hustlers. After trying to get his money back, he swipes a strongbox from the crooks, which contains a pistol and (though he doesn't realize this until later) several thousand dollars. This motivates the two crooks to pursue him and sets up the film's clumsy climax.

Bridges happens into a desert where a Hollywood unit happens to be on location filming a Western. (The same thing happened to Eleanor Boardman in *Souls For Sale,* back in 1923.) He tags along with them to Los Angeles and is soon working as an extra in Western films. From this he graduates to stunt work and is on the verge of being turned into an honest-to-goodness Western actor. But he holds out for too much money ($150 a week) and gets fired. Still, his dream is to become a writer and he shows his unpublished manuscript to Andy Griffith, in the role of a has-been actor AND writer who now does stunt work. Griffith tries to claim the manuscript as his own, but eventually relents and comes to Bridges's rescue when the two Nevada crooks close in on the hapless young writer.

However hokey the story, *Hearts of the West* had a simple charm about it, thanks in some measure to the winning performances by Bridges and Griffith, and also to a hilarious spoof of the classic 1930s director, played expertly by Alan Arkin.

But the movie failed to find favor with audiences and was soon forgotten. Perhaps it failed because it was more sentimental than outrageous, aiming for warmth rather than belly laughs.

Peter Bogdanovich, an acknowledged worshipper of early Hollywood, took the latter course — aiming for big laughs — in his next film, released late in 1976 and titled *Nickelodeon.*

Heading the cast were Ryan O'Neal as a novice lawyer who stumbles into film directing back in the early silent era; Burt Reynolds as a roustabout who becomes a film actor; and Tatum O'Neal as a young country girl who keeps rescuing the bumbling filmmakers. Also featured was Brian Keith, overacting atrociously in the role of an early movie mogul.

Whatever merit the film may have had in depicting the struggles of filmmaking pioneers was dissipated by Bogdanovich's insistence on cramming as much slapstick into the film as one would expect in a Chaplin or Keaton compilation feature. For the first half hour or so, it seemed no actor or actress in the cast could walk ten paces without tripping, falling, pulling down a set, or bumping into somebody else who was equally incapable of navigating.

Hearts of the West. Up to his neck in water and pulp fiction was Jeff Bridges, as a would-be writer of Westerns in this nostalgic glance at Hollywood in the thirties. (MGM, 1976)

Nickelodeon. Ryan O'Neal, with megaphone, played a silent era director. Driving the truck is Tatum O'Neal. The Peter Bogdanovich touch pervaded the whole film, as light as a concrete feather. (Columbia, 1976)

Another serious flaw was the murkiness of the Tatum O'Neal role. Even allowing for that young actress's remarkable screen presence, Tatum's appearance in the cast of *Nickelodeon* seemed to be justified only by the fact that her famous father was the star of the film. One can understand Bogdanovich's temptation to team the O'Neals (they had done well for him in *Paper Moon* a few years before) but it seems a pity that a better role could not have been created for her.

A far more grim and disturbing bit of nostalgia was *Inserts* (1976), written and directed by John Byrum and starring Richard Dreyfuss as a Boy Wonder director of the silent era fallen on hard times due to the introduction of sound and reduced to making porno films to stay alive.

There was sardonic humor as well as a dark side to this small and inexpensive film, all shot on one set and with a cast of only five players. Dreyfuss, in a sensitive and haunting performance, becomes almost a symbol of Hollywood failure — the need to do distasteful work, the proud but fading memory of grander days, the bitterness of reality, the loneliness of a near-genius no longer able to cope with a world he finds alien.

Inserts had its sensational side, too. Over Dreyfuss's angry objections, it was X-rated for its harsh language and inclusion of some raunchy sex scenes. But many critics saw in it far more merit than one might expect in a typical "sexploitation" porno flick, and both the Dreyfuss acting and the Byrum direction tended to support that argument.

But the film attracted relatively little attention and slipped into that limbo reserved for movies that are neither as blatantly commercial as *Nickelodeon* nor as irresistably salacious as standard hard-core porno flicks that make big money.

The very fact that *Inserts* was made at all indicates the extent to which movie nostalgia had become a marketable product by the mid-1970s. It failed commercially, to be sure, but obviously its backers must have thought it had a chance of success.

Nor was *Inserts* the only "small" picture of the mid-1970s to deal, one way or another, with Hollywood nostalgia.

There was, for instance, a generally worthless quickie called *Train Ride to Hollywood,* featuring a musical group called Bloodstone. They played a pop music group one of whose members (Harry Williams, Jr.) is so devoted to old movies that he has a dream in which the group achieves Hollywood stardom. The film used look-alikes for various old-time stars in its attempt to cash in on the nostalgia tide.

There was *Gosh!,* a raunchy sexploitation comedy in which Sharon Kelly, as a Hollywood waitress, provides sexual services for various filmland types to further her acting ambitions.

There was *Hollywood Blue,* a compilation of stag film footage clearly intended only for porno houses — yet again being "topical" by focussing on Hollywood nostalgia.

And there was *Hollywood Boulevard,* a paean to the B-movie and something of a compendium of B-movie clichés. Made for a remarkable $60,000,

Inserts. **The leering, unshaven, bathrobed man behind the camera is Richard Dreyfuss, who played an over-age Boy Wonder reduced to filming pornos. (United Artists, 1976)**

Hollywood Boulevard. **Four Hollywood hopefuls smile for the camera in this sly and generally unheralded "salute" to B movies. (New World Pictures, 1976)**

the New World Pictures release concerned a star-struck young girl (Candice Rialson) trying to get a break in Hollywood. Her adventures, often hilarious, range from doing stunt work to witnessing an on-set murder. All of this is done tongue-in-cheek and with an intentional lack of slickness to point up the small-budget nature of this film designed to poke fun at the small-budget world it recalls.

It remained for Mel Brooks to make the ultimate statement on Hollywood nostalgia — on film. This was his 1976 film, *Silent Movie,* an attempt to revive both the sight gags of the soundless days and the hectic pace of the early studios. Brooks played a down-at-the-heels director trying to get his career going again. He convinces a studio to finance his venture: a silent movie. Despite the attempts of a villainous conglomerate to sabotage Brooks's film, he signs a string of big name stars (Burt Reynolds, James Caan, Paul Newman, Anne Bancroft, Liza Minelli) to work in his film. His loyal sidekicks are played by Marty Feldman and Dom De Luise.

With all this going for him, Brooks took the idea one step further: although set in 1976, *Silent Movie* was made as a silent. That is, there are sound effects galore and a musical score, but no dialogue. Brooks wanted to prove that visual comedy was still the best. Only title cards were used to carry necessary dialogue — in print.

To what extent Brooks succeeded artistically is debatable. Riding high after such successes as *Blazing Saddles* and *Young Frankenstein,* he had by now built a substantial following for his erratic but often hilarious movies. Inevitably, the loyal Brooks fans tended to love *Silent Movie.* Others, less slavishly devoted to the Brooks style, were not amused. Still, largely because of the Brooks reputation, and, no doubt, partly because of the sustained public fascination with movie nostalgia, *Silent Movie* was a smash hit: it returned a whopping $20,000,000 in its first year of release.

The center of an even more loyal army of fans was the equally distinctive Woody Allen, and in

Silent Movie. **Mel Brooks, riding the camera crane, was behind this speechless spoof of the silent era updated. (20th Century-Fox, 1976)**

1976, he, too, turned his attention to an aspect of Hollywood-related nostalgia.

This was *The Front*, a glance back at the Joe McCarthy era in the 1950s, when Red-baiting was the national pastime and blacklists ruled the studios. That Woody Allen and the others connected with this film should decide to tackle such a subject can surely be regarded as admirable. What they did with it, however, is something else again.

The Front was written by Walter Bernstein, produced and directed by Martin Ritt, and its cast included Zero Mostel and Herschel Bernardi. As it happens all these men (and far, far more) were themselves blacklisted in those dark days when the reckless, ruthless senator from Wisconsin made his national reputation by destroying the careers of often innocent people he decided were Communists or "fellow-travelers."

(A 1977 television documentary-type drama, *Tail-Gunner Joe*, pretty well covered the McCarthy story, and numerous books on the era are available, most notably a biography written by Richard Rovere.)

McCarthy did not, of course, invent witch hunts. In the late 1940s and early 1950s, the same game was played by the House Un-American Activities Committee of the U.S. Congress, and this august body turned its attention to Hollywood in what was surely one of the most bizarre public inquiries ever held. Various anti-Communist zealots also climbed on the bandwagon and the end result of all this frantic searching under beds for Reds was The Blacklist — several blacklists, in fact, but all of them achieving the same effect, namely throwing out of work actors, writers, musicians, artists, directors, and anyone else "suspected" of favoring communism.

Actors in films, radio, and television found

The Front. Blacklisted television writer Michael Murphy turns to his friend, Woody Allen, for help in this unsatisfying examination of McCarthy era excesses. (Columbia, 1976)

themselves unemployed and unemployable, simply because his or her name had turned up on somebody's list of undesirables. In a way, they were perhaps the hardest hit, because they were too well-known (by name and face) to get around the blacklist. Many writers, however, managed to keep working by the devious method of using pseudonyms. Hollywood was not up to defying the witchhunters, but it was not above buying a script (usually at a reduced rate) from a blacklisted writer — provided his real name did not appear on it.

It was this aspect of the McCarthy era that *The Front* chose to tackle. But it was a rather clumsy tackle, groping aimlessly for black humor in what was a big enough subject to warrant a far more intelligent effort.

Woody Allen played a brainless nonentity whose friend (Michael Murphy) is a writer who finds himself blacklisted. In order to survive, he arranges to have Woody's name (the character played by Allen is named Harold Prince) appear on his scripts — in exchange for ten percent of the selling price. In time, Murphy realizes he has created a monster: his witless friend begins to complain that the scripts bearing his name must improve. When "the front" (Woody) is himself investigated, we realize that he really doesn't understand much of what is going on, and even his brief denunciation of the investigative committee seems a limp and pointless ending.

The Front failed both as comedy (its surface appeal, and the quality one expected from a Woody Allen) and, worse still, as a serious attempt to come to grips with the ugly issue of blacklisting — and especially blacklisting in Hollywood.

Rather than dealing with blacklisting in the movie industry, the movie industry chose to throw stones at the television industry. *The Front* was set in New York, its blacklisted writer was a television writer, its executives who bowed to the pressure of witch-hunters were television executives. Nary a mention that the same thing went on (to an equal or greater extent) in the Hollywood film studios.

Ironically, television had already done its own *mea culpa* bit a year before. CBS presented a television drama called *Fear On Trial,* based on the blacklisting of John Henry Faulk, a 1950s radio personality who was hounded out of broadcasting by witchhunters. Faulk had the courage and determination to fight the blacklist and he ultimately won his court case — though no money to

speak of. The network which had eased him off the air was CBS — the same one which, two decades later, presented the Faulk drama and even identified itself as the network guilty of wronging him.

But no young filmgoer seeing *The Front* would suspect from it that the Hollywood feature film studios were at least as guilty of cooperating with the blacklist as the broadcasting networks were.

(An observer can hardly resist noting the movie industry's courage when it comes to criticizing television. The 1976 feature film, *Network,* attacked with unseemly relish the excesses of television's handling of news. This film, from an original story by Paddy Chayefsky, flailed a wide brush in denouncing the total absence of moral and ethical standards in the television networks' manipulation of audiences. Few Hollywood portrayals of movie moguls have been as sinister as the television tycoons depicted in *Network.*)

Despite some box-office evidence that the Hollywood nostalgia boom had peaked (*Hearts of the West* and *Won Ton Ton, The Dog Who Saved Hollywood* were both financial disasters, and even *That's Entertainment, Part 2* was a long way from achieving the financial success of its earlier namesake), yet one more big budget movie dealing with an earlier Hollywood was in the works.

Sam Spiegel, producer of such outstanding films as *The Bridge on the River Kwai, On the Waterfront,* and *The African Queen,* decided to turn his attention to a Hollywood story. At first, he planned to use some autobiographical material, but instead he turned to F. Scott Fitzgerald's un-

The Last Tycoon. Robert DeNiro was F. Scott Fitzgerald's tragic hero in this reverent but lifeless film version of Fitzgerald's unfinished work. (Paramount, 1976)

finished novel, *The Last Tycoon*. He engaged Elia Kazan to direct, and Harold Pinter to do the screenplay. It was to be an ambitious film (budgeted at some $6,000,000) with Robert De Niro heading the cast.

De Niro would play Monroe Stahr, the Fitzgerald character supposedly modeled after Irving Thalberg, MGM's boy genius who made some of that studio's most impressive films in the 1930s. (Thalberg was in his mid-30s when he died, and is still revered by movie old-timers.)

But Fitzgerald, who had drunk himself into obscurity during the years he spent in Hollywood, died before he could complete *The Last Tycoon*. Over the years, there had often been talk of a film based on the Fitzgerald book, but until now it was only talk.

When the film finally emerged, late in 1976, there was polite praise for De Niro's performance as Stahr, but not much else. Some critics felt the Spiegel-Pinter-Kazan version had "missed" the essence of Fitzgerald's writing. Others argued that the Fitzgerald novel, unfinished as it was and written when the novelist was on the skids, was hardly worth the effort.

Even with a name-heavy cast (Jack Nicholson, Tony Curtis, Robert Mitchum, Jeanne Moreau) *The Last Tycoon* drew yawns. At least two critics headlined their reviews: "A Stahr Is Stillborn."*

But Hollywood, ever the land of me-too-ism, has a tougher time stopping trends than starting them.

*1976 also brought a new remake of *A Star Is Born*, with Barbra Streisand and Kris Kristofferson, but its milieu was totally changed from moviemaking to the rock music scene, so it scarcely belongs in the present survey.

More movie movies were either in production or in the planning stages in the spring of 1977.

Rudolph Valentino and Marilyn Monroe, two standbys for dissectors of glamour, were due for further examinations. Neil Simon was reported working on something to be called *Bogart Slept Here*. Another project supposedly in the works was titled *Tom Mix Died For Your Sins*. Glenda Jackson and Carol Burnet were reportedly signed to appear together in *Two Gals From Topeka*, about a couple of Kansas waitresses who head for Hollywood in the 1930s. *The Fan Club*, based on a sizzling Harold Robbins book, was due for filming. So was a film biography of Bill (Bojangles) Robinson.

When Sam Spiegel was making *The Last Tycoon*, he responded in an interview to the ancient charge that movies about Hollywood are supposed to be box-office poison.

"Rubbish," Spiegel was quoted as saying. "Bad movies about Hollywood are unsuccessful. But films like *The Bad and the Beautiful* and *A Star Is Born* have been terrific hits. There is no reason why a film about Hollywood shouldn't sell. This town has been the symbol of glamor for generations, and there is a great nostalgia for that part of people's past."

Despite the dubious fate of his own entry into the nostalgia sweepstakes, Spiegel's argument still held some validity in 1977. Hollywood's future still seemed to lie in its past. Audiences still seemed eager to be shown again and told again what a glamorous, nutty, greedy, corrupt, decadent, irresistible place Hollywood was . . . and maybe still is.